WIRED TO WIN

BILL RITCHIE

HARVEST◆HOUSE PUBLISHERS

WIRED TO WIN

Copyright © 1993 by Harvest House Publishers
Eugene, Oregon 97402

Library of Congress Cataloging-in-Publication Data

Ritchie, Bill.
    Wired to win / Bill Ritchie.
       p.   cm.
    ISBN 1-56507-042-9
    1. Identification (Religion).   2. Success—Religious aspects—Christianity. I. Title.
    BV4509.5.R53   1993
    248.4—dc20   92-35347
                                             CIP

Have you ever looked at another Christian and, with a sigh, thought, *If only I could be like him*, or, *If only I had what she has, then . . .*

Then what? If you grasp what Bill Ritchie is proposing in *Wired to Win* (and he makes it easy and delightful to do so), the sighs will stop. "If onlys" won't even be considered because you'll understand that, in His own unique and perfect way, God has wired you to be a winner—not a winner in the world's substandard way of thinking, but a winner in God's eyes.

Readers might be startled by some of the terms Bill uses to make his points, but they will find that his words are meant to take the reader beyond watered-down phrases to the clarion call of our Lord. Those who would follow our Lord are to love Him supremely so that every other relationship would seem as hatred in comparison.

Above all, Bill's message is biblical. He lauds the apostle Paul, who he says was "never one to be caught up in the fads of the moment, no matter how spiritual those fads appeared; Paul brought everything back to the Word for evaluation." Bill encourages you to do the same thing.

This book is filled with colorful, detailed, and varied stories of people from all walks of life—stories that will light your fire, stir up the gifts within you, and give you the affirmation that God has wired *you* to win!

—Kay Arthur
Precept Ministries

_A C K N O W L E D G M E N T S_

Without any question, I have been greatly influenced by people who are wired to win and are winning. There are a number of them in my own church congregation. You'll read their stories in this book. But there are other winners I'd like to mention now who have blessed me immeasurably.

Two particular men have made a huge impact on my life. Dr. Joe A. Harding both led me to the Lord and nurtured me in my calling to be a pastor. Not only was he there when I discovered how I was wired, but he also enabled me to keep my focus during my college and graduate-school years when so many other enticing options for my life presented themselves.

As I matured in the Lord, pastor Chuck Smith of Calvary Chapel, Costa Mesa, served to set the pace for a ministry that was truly Word-centered. His faithfulness to center his life and teaching on God's Word—and his steadfast refusal to get caught up in the fads and fancies of the day—has really helped me to understand what winning is all about. In a crowd of winners, Chuck stands out!

It is to these winners that I dedicate this book. God bless you for your faithfulness to be everything God designed you to be, and to do everything He called you to do!

CONTENTS

WIRED TO WIN

Wired to Win!

It seems as if it happened yesterday. Though it took place when I was just ten years old, the emotions aren't hard to recapture. It was that traumatic.

Sometime during the spring of my fourth-grade year, I decided to embark on a new adventure. A beautiful roller-skating rink opened across town and I decided to get serious about the art of skating. Why not? Skateland was a beautiful place, filled with people having fun. Since the floor was brand-new, there were no nicks or warped spots to trip you up. What a great place to spend my spare time!

I soon talked my mom into dropping me off there on several successive Saturdays. It was the perfect way to discover whether skating was truly my cup of tea.

It didn't take me long to get hooked. Why, you could glide around the floor at what seemed to be a hundred miles an hour! Sure, sometimes you knocked somebody over and maybe you got clipped yourself. But it was still lots more fun than riding my bike around the neighborhood with my trusty bulldog Muggs.

Several weeks of skating quickly made it clear that rental skates did not allow me to go as fast nor do as many quick stops as the folks who had their own skates. They could turn on a dime and screech to a halt much more quickly than I could. I just *had* to get my own skates!

Luckily for me, my birthday was just a couple of months away. I spent hours talking with the salesman at the roller rink, figuring out what kind of skates would be best for me. Even though I was just ten years old, already I was an old hand at chatting with people. I came by it naturally—my dad could talk to a tree and it would talk back! And I was a chip off the old block—make that a "chunk" off the old block. Like my dad, I was about as wide as I was tall. Not to worry: With the right skates, that wouldn't make any difference. Now all I had to do was start dropping hints.

I'm not sure what I said, but somehow my parents took the hints and gave me exactly the skates I wanted. More than that, they even came in a beautiful red suitcase that fit them precisely. I hadn't even asked for that. Wow, was I ever lucky!

I couldn't wait to get to the rink. I knew it would be just like buying a new pair of tennis shoes. I always could run faster when my tennies were new. Likewise, I would now enjoy an entirely new dimension of skating. I almost hesitated to put them on, not wanting to mar the pristine wheels. But then, they were going to have to hit the deck sometime, so I put them on my feet. Perfect! They were exactly what I needed, as if they had been constructed from molds taken right off my feet.

When I glided onto the floor, it was as if everyone else vanished. It was now just me and my new skates. They didn't squeak. They didn't hesitate. They didn't stick. They just rolled effortlessly and smoothly across the floor. Nothing could stop me now!

As autumn rolled around and I moved into fifth grade, a whole new door opened to me. Skateland offered classes to teach you how to *really* skate. They said they would teach you how to do figures like the ice skaters you see in the Olympics, how to do dances with partners, and present a better overall approach to the art of skating. If you signed up for Saturday lessons to take place during the school year, you were guaranteed to move far beyond what you might manage on your own. After conferring with my folks, I signed up.

The lessons were just as advertised. Although my excess poundage made some of the steps tougher for me to negotiate, still I got better week by week. But that's not the best part. Unbeknownst to me, one of the cutest girls in my fifth-grade class had also signed up for these lessons. I quickly and delightedly calculated that I would be with her every Saturday for the whole year. Skating was definitely for me!

As we approached the end of the year, it was announced that we were going to take part in a contest. Some judges from other rinks were to spend a Saturday watching all of us do the moves we had learned. They would give us points on how well we performed each of the compulsory figures, the dance steps, and our general skating technique. Depending on how many points we earned, we would get either a certificate, a trophy, or the grand prize.

The thought of such a contest made me anxious. Certainly, I could skate. I could keep up with most of the kids in my class. But my size made some of the steps tricky for me. A move that was no big deal for others was a real challenge for me. Yet I hoped that if I gave it my best shot, perhaps I could at least get one of the small trophies. Probably not the grand prize—but who knows?

Finally the big day came. Like all the other kids, my nerves were on edge. I was sweating as I put on my skates—not because I was hot, but because I was worried. I so wanted to do well! Happily, when I moved onto the floor, I felt good. I seemed to be moving well. It just seemed to be "one of those days." How fortuitous!

As the day progressed, I moved from event to event and did each of the figures in order. Amazingly, I was able to do some steps that I wasn't sure I could perform. I was on my way now! Why settle for a little trophy? Why not go for the grand prize?

We broke for lunch and then resumed our competition. It was great. I was feeling better all the time. I just knew that something super was going to happen.

When it was all over and we were awaiting word from the judges, already I was pondering how I was going to respond when I was awarded the grand prize. Visions popped into my head of what people said when they received an Oscar. "Thank you, parents. Thank you, teachers. Thank you, dog. Thank..."

We all sat on benches facing a table on the skating floor which was filled with certificates and trophies. As our names were called based on our points, we would skate out to meet the judges, pick up whatever we had earned, and then skate back to our places.

They started with those who had earned only a certificate. You could tell by their faces that they were disappointed, but tried their best to smile. They rolled out and got their certificates and then skated back to their places. One by one they were called. And, one by one, I knew that I was moving up the ranks.

As they moved through the trophy winners, eventually there were only a couple of us left. I knew it! I just knew it! They were going to call out the last kid's name and give him a trophy; then I would get the grand prize.

I was absolutely unprepared for what happened next.

They called the other kid's name, all right. But when he skated out, they gave him the grand prize, thanked everybody for taking part, and dismissed us.

Wait a minute! What about me? I didn't get the grand prize; I didn't get a trophy; I didn't even score enough points to earn a certificate. I was the only kid in the whole class who got nothing. I was stunned...shocked...speechless. While everybody around me was talking, laughing, and comparing awards, I was silent. Truly, I was in a class by myself—the bottom class. A class for rejects, for losers, for kids too heavy for skating who can't make all the right moves. I desperately wanted to cry, but I was too big. Still, I had to get out of there.

I slowly skated over to an area where nobody was sitting. I took off my skates—the skates that a few hours before had meant so much to me. I carefully put them into their little red suitcase. I locked the suitcase . . . and never opened it again.

Do you know what it's like to be shut out? Do you know what it feels like to want desperately to win and yet lose? Do you know what it's like to try something and fail?

Unless I miss my guess, you do. No doubt, somewhere along the line, you have desired to win at something but haven't been able to. Maybe you have figuratively put your skates in your suitcase, locked it up, and never opened it again. It isn't fun to lose. Nobody likes to lose. Everybody likes to win.

It's just that simple. That's why we exalt winners. That's why we want to rub shoulders with the rich, the famous, and the talented. Maybe something will rub off. And maybe, just maybe, if we try hard enough, we can be winners, too.

Well, I've got news for you. Whether you know it or not, *you have been wired to win*! So has everyone you know. You may not feel that way and your experience may tell you something quite different, but the fact is, the One who put you together designed you to win!

Over the course of the pages that follow, I want to help you begin to do just that. At the very least, I want to point you in the right direction. And I don't want you ever to lock your skates away!

How do I intend to do this? I assure you it isn't by means of some come-on telling you to "do three things and you'll be healthy, wealthy, and wise." Instead, I plan to do it by helping you understand what *real* winning is all about. Once I do that, I intend to encourage you to do it.

I'll be introducing you to folks I know who either have won or are in the process of winning. You will find them to be quite different from each other. Some of them are financially comfortable, while others have little; some are well-known, others aren't known beyond their own neighborhoods; some are highly educated, while others have graduated summa cum laude from the school of hard knocks. In many ways, these folks are completely dissimilar to one another.

At the same time, one thing unites them all: They are winners. They all have been wired to win, and they all are winning.

One of them may be quite a bit like you. I hope so! That's why I've included so many of them and why they come from such diverse backgrounds and experiences. It is my deepest desire that you will become so caught up in what has captivated them that it will grab you, too.

To lay my cards right on the table, I really hope that you become a whole new chapter. When you do write your own story, send me a copy. I'd love to read it!

Follow carefully what you are about to read. And give yourself permission to become hopelessly lost in winning. Nobody is more wired to win than you are. Did you catch that? *Nobody is more wired to win than you are*—nobody. Hang on! Let me tell you why.

Discover How You Are Wired

*The man
who has meditated on himself
for a certain length of time comes back
to life sensing the position he
can occupy. Then he can
act effectively.*

—Henri Matisse

Years ago a saying was floating around that insisted, "You are a jewel, unique and priceless, a joy in someone's heart. I don't care how you feel about it, believe it. God don't make no junk!"

Regardless of the skewed grammar, the statement is true. You are precious, one-of-a-kind, distinctive, invaluable. God doesn't create junk! He has made you in a unique, particular way. That is why it is so critical to discover how you are wired.

Unfortunately, it's easy to be simplistic in this process of exploration. In much of today's evangelical subculture, for example, your identity is often reduced to your spiritual gift(s).

15

From Paul's discussion of spiritual gifts in his letters to the Romans, the Corinthians, and the Ephesians, it is argued that:

- everybody has a spiritual gift or gifts
- spiritual gifts are given by God to be used
- therefore, your role or identity in the body of Christ is a function of whatever gift(s) God has built into your life.

Thus, according to this scheme of things, if you have the gift of service, you are a servant. You find your fulfillment in serving others. If you have the gift of prophecy, you are a prophet. You find your fulfillment in exposing and expounding God's truth. And on the theory goes.

Now there is no question that if you are a believer you do have a spiritual gift or gifts. You can figure out what they are by taking a test, going through a seminar, reflecting on the Word, asking a friend, or a variety of other methods. But contrary to what many people teach, once you have determined your spiritual gift(s), you have only *begun* to discern your wiring. That is only one of the things God has built into your life; it is not all!

This subject of spiritual gifts is discussed in a number of well-developed books. If this is an area where you need some guidance, I suggest you read one of the fine works mentioned at the end of the chapter.[1] But for our purposes here, it will be much more helpful to look at some of the other things included in your wiring—items that are all too often overlooked. If you're ever going to win, you need to deal with them all.

Is IQ the Same as Intelligence?

God has woven your life together like a beautiful, multicolored, multitextured tapestry. As you begin to examine the warp and woof of your own fabric, you need first to consider your intelligence. Make no mistake about it. You have been constructed with a particular intelligence which you can either use to its fullest capacity or neglect and allow to atrophy.

Intelligence quotient (IQ), the significant number that figuratively was stamped on your forehead as a schoolchild, has been a source of confusion and frustration for many people. Intended as a tool for comparison, it has been used variously as a pigeonhole, an excuse, a weapon, and a badge.

Theoretically (and it *is* theory) the IQ is a measure of your intellectual potential. Although universally accepted by the population at large, professional educators, psychologists, and psychiatrists disagree on the validity of the very concept of IQ. They argue that it is far too simplistic to imagine that a variety of tests could determine the true range of a person's intellectual abilities.

One of the leading assailants of the concept of IQ is psychiatrist Paul Pearsall. He writes,

> The dominance of the testing movement in our society has seduced us into thinking that test scores "are" potential. Test scores are simply numbers used to arrange people in order from "less to more" on some arbitrary scale. Aptitude tests are not "apt to do" tests at all, but they do become "ought to do" tests. If Albert Einstein, one of the greatest geniuses of our time, were to take a test to measure his potential, it is likely we would find that he had no potential at all. Einstein failed miserably on simple tests, and simple arithmetic baffled him. There is not a test that could measure the "potential" of an Einstein, and there are no tests that could measure [any child's] potential. . . . People are constantly changing, and there is no single factor that predicts brilliance of any type.[2]

Reducing someone's intelligence potential to a quotient is not only simplistic, it is misleading. As Harvard's Howard Gardner reveals in his fascinating book *Frames of Mind*, each person possesses a blend of at least *five* kinds of intelligence! He writes:

My review of earlier studies of intelligence and cognition has suggested the existence of a number of different intellectual strengths, or competences [*sic*], each of which may have its own developmental history. The review of recent work in neurobiology has again suggested the presence of areas in the brain that correspond, at least roughly, to certain forms of cognition; and these same studies imply a neural organization that proves hospitable to the notion of different modes of information processing. At least in the fields of psychology and neurobiology, the *Zeitgeist* appears primed for the identification of several human intellectual competences [*sic*].[3]

On the basis of his studies in the field, Gardner presents a persuasive argument that there is much evidence for

the existence of several relatively autonomous human intellectual competences [*sic*], [or] "human intelligences." The exact nature and breadth of each intellectual "frame" has not so far been satisfactorily established, nor has the precise number of intelligences been fixed. But the conviction that there exist at least some intelligences, that these are relatively independent of one another, and that they can be fashioned and combined in a multiplicity of adaptive ways by individuals and cultures, seems to me to be increasingly difficult to deny.[4]

In *Frames of Mind*, Gardner delineates five kinds of intelligence, including linguistic intelligence, musical intelligence, logical-mathematical intelligence, spatial intelligence, and bodily-kinesthetic intelligence. In later works, he expands that, suggesting that there are others yet to be discovered. Regardless of the specific number of "intelligences," the key here is that each person possesses a unique *blend* of them. Hence, it is simply misleading to reduce your intelligence to an IQ test.

You have intelligence, all right. But exactly what that is, how it is determined, and how you deploy it (or them, as the case may be) is an entirely different matter.

Reducing intelligence to IQ not only misses its complexity, it also ignores the way your intelligence functions. Each of us processes information uniquely. For instance, researchers tell us that some people are primarily auditory learners. They learn best by listening. While charts, graphs, and visuals on a board may be interesting, they are not nearly as helpful to such persons as are verbal explanations. On the other hand, a person may be a visual learner. For him, a picture truly is worth a thousand words. An explanation may be interesting, but seeing increases his understanding far more.

This concept isn't easy for some people to grasp. A few years ago one of my sons had a music teacher who was accustomed to training highly gifted students. As a means of introducing a new piece to a student, her practice was to play a recording of the new piece as recorded by some concert artist. That way the student had a good idea of what the finished product was supposed to sound like.

While this was helpful for most students, the teacher quickly decided it was *too* helpful for my son Jason. Because he learned auditorily, and because he had absolute pitch, he could learn a song just by listening to the music. Seeing the musical score was not nearly as important to him as hearing it. It took his teacher a while to catch on, but once she did, she didn't like it. If Jason asked her to repeat the playing of a piece, she responded, "No, I won't play it again. If I do, then you will know how to play it just from listening. That's not the way I want you to learn."

What she said was absolutely true. Jason *did* learn from listening. And there was no question he also needed to learn how to play from reading the printed page. But my son felt his teacher was penalizing him because of the way he happened to be wired to learn. While his experience was unfortunate, it is all too common. Though we often act and try to teach otherwise, we don't all process information in exactly the same way.

How Many 80-Year-Olds
Play in the Big Leagues?

What other factors besides intelligence affect your wiring? How about your age? How much water has passed under the bridge in your life?

God asked the 80-year-old Moses to lead His people out of captivity in Egypt—not to pole-vault in the Olympics! Different ages are better suited for different tasks. For example, experts tell us that the easiest time to learn foreign languages is before the age of six. Hence, if you're 50 and you speak only your mother tongue, God probably hasn't wired you to find your fulfillment translating Scripture for some unreached people group on one of Indonesia's 3000-plus islands. On the other hand, Scripture clearly admonishes the older to teach the younger. So without a few extra candles on your birthday cake, you don't qualify for the latter job!

Experience

Then there is experience. Certainly that is an important facet of your wiring. A moment's reflection will tell you that experience varies greatly even among people of the same age. And all those experiences are pointing in a particular direction. By the time I was 26, for example, I had earned a doctorate in religion, had earned a certificate in a graduate school in Switzerland, had lived in four countries and studied (to some degree) four different languages, had pastored a church by myself, and had been a full-time assistant professor in a state university. I also was a husband, father, and homeowner.

Whether that was a lot or a little is beside the point. Experience is not a "better than/worse than" proposition; it is just "different than." My personal experiences accomplished some specific things that brought me to a certain point in my life, and God used those experiences to fashion my future in a distinct way. In the same way, God has given you very particular experiences to equip you for what lies ahead.

Experience includes education and training. What kind of formal education have you had? How much of it? Good or bad? What has on-the-job training prepared you to do?

I find it fascinating to follow the life and ministry of the apostle Paul and see how he was prepared academically and intellectually for the rigors to come. A man without his training would not have been able to deal with the challenges that confronted him. Because of his education and training, however, the process of critical thought, analysis, and debate came quite naturally to him.

Of course it's not necessary for you to pile up several letters behind your name for God to be able to use you mightily, but you must not shy away from diligent, formal study if your wiring requires it.

Situation in Life

Another intriguing part of your wiring related to your experience is your situation in life. Where are you right now? What mix of circumstances confronts you? Although you may not be comfortable with your current situation, it might be exactly the spot where God intends to use you, the place in which you will find your greatest fulfillment.

Years ago I knew a truck driver. When he became a Christian, he was highly effective at reaching people for the Lord. It was not at all unusual for him to lead six or seven people to the Lord in a week in the course of his truck driving. He picked up hitchhikers along the way, spoke to servers in restaurants, and witnessed to the personnel in the weigh stations along the interstate. He enjoyed a unique and powerful ability to help people see their need for Jesus.

As he grew in his faith, he got the notion that if he was *really* going to serve God, he needed to be a professional clergyman. He needed to quit driving his 18-wheeler and go to school to learn how to preach or teach or whatever it was that pastors did.

Unfortunately, this did not *at all* suit his style or training. It didn't mesh with his natural inclination. And it opposed his situation in life. But it was the only image he had had presented to him. So with that in mind, he quit his job and began attending a small Christian training center to start his preparation for professional ministry.

As you might guess, disaster was the result. My friend flailed around like a fish out of water. He grew frustrated by the academic environment and discouraged by the lack of joy he found in witnessing. He had believed a misconception about *real* ministry and had not taken into account his situation in life. As a result, his effectiveness in ministry nose-dived, as did his joy and enthusiasm. All because he didn't take seriously something as simple as his situation in life.

Don't sell this aspect short! Are you a single parent, with some specific challenges that need to be addressed in whatever life path you choose? Are your credit cards tapped out? Are you engaged and contemplating marriage, but haven't thought seriously about how your fiancée fits into your future? Just what is your situation in life? What is it telling you about where you are supposed to be?

Heritage

You also possess a specific heritage that has shaped your life. This facet is so important I deal with it in depth in another book, *A Dad Who Loves You* (Multnomah Press, 1992). For better or worse, several factors have influenced you: relationships with parents; living situations and conditions when you grew up; the way you were taught, trained, disciplined and loved (or neglected). If you don't think heritage is all that important, consider this: Criminologist James Wilson and psychologist Richard Herrnstein, in a ten-year study, concluded that individual moral choices are most profoundly shaped *through family influence* by the time a person is six years of age![5] Yes, your heritage is a critical aspect of your wiring.

Race

Another factor in the mix is race. Regardless of how politically correct, tolerant, or enlightened we strive to be, racial differences are a fact of life. Tour a large city from Little Italy to Chinatown and you will realize that the great American melting pot is not as homogenized as we would like to think. It's more like a huge salad bowl. The same is true in most nations of the world where large populations of immigrants have settled. Like it or not, race is a factor in your wiring, and while it should never be an inhibitor to doing any and everything that God created you to do, it does play into the way you have been put together. To assume it is irrelevant is to miss one of your distinctives!

Gender

Gender is another issue in your wiring (or should I say "plumbing"?). I maintain there really is a difference between the sexes. Unless my wife and I have been greatly deceived, we were put together *quite* differently—at least it sure looked that way the last time I checked. And I for one greatly enjoy the difference. I celebrate our distinctives!

Significant differences between males and females exist in everything from relative body fat content to the ability to tolerate pain. And that is an important facet of how you are wired. You ignore it to your own detriment.

Marital Status

Another aspect of your wiring is your marital status. Time and again this is overlooked, but it is integral to who you are. The Bible teaches that when two become one in marriage, something extraordinary takes place on a spiritual level. Because that "something" is not a physical change and therefore not visible, it's easy to assume nothing has happened except for a legal commitment. In truth, however, God has taken what once were two unique, separate individuals, each with his/her own rights, and fused them together. Their individual expressions become unified.

Thus, if you are married, your ultimate development depends on how your wiring interacts with that of your spouse. If he/she is not in sync with the way you see things coming together, the two of you will need to adjust. To be sure, your spouse may simply be stubborn, wrong, ignorant, or off the track in some other way. But that person is still your spouse, still that other part of you. You must take this into account as you consider how you have been put together and how you are going to function best.

Similarly, the fact that you might be single is also relevant. A friend of mine has considered pastoring a church, but he would never act on that idea apart from being married. Why not? Because he feels that, for him, it would be unproductive to pastor as a single man. While you might not share his conviction, you still need to understand that your marital status is a part of the mix of who you are.

Talents and Abilities

That mix is significantly impacted by your talents and abilities. Unquestionably you have particular skills, abilities, and talents. Although they may not be the ones you want, they are the ones you have. You may be especially talented in woodworking, or you may have powerful gifts in the kitchen. You may be multitalented, able to do lots of things well, and have a hard time confining yourself to one or two areas. But if you *are* multitalented, why *should* you confine yourself? Doesn't that variety of talents express the way in which you have been created?

Whatever your talents, skills, and abilities, they have been built into your life for good reason. They weren't meant to be rejected or hidden; they were meant to be developed and utilized for the glory of God.

Passion

Another crucial ingredient in discovering the way you are wired is your passion. What do you like to do? What do you seem to be naturally drawn to? What really gets you going? It is highly unlikely that God has designed you to be or do something you hate. Do you really believe God expects you to win, to find your fulfillment and joy in an arena which nauseates you? Is that what you find in the Bible?

As you page through the Scriptures, you find the "winners" fully developing the facets of their lives that God built in from the beginning. Peter was designed with a bent toward leading, and that is what he did. John had a rational mind that explained well the various aspects of faith, and that is what he did. Noah was a man of faith who was good at tending to details. Review sometime the specific instructions he received for building his floating zoo, and decide whether he was the man for the job!

Though you may never have thought about it, you already have within a deep desire to be and do that which God has designed you to be. You just need to allow yourself to focus on it.

Disabilities

A facet of your wiring you may never have considered is your disabilities. Our culture's obsession with perfection makes it easy to assume that disabilities are disqualifiers. But God can work around and through disabilities, and we must allow Him to do so. If you are blind, you probably won't fly a plane for Mission Aviation Fellowship. But you may run the entire operation from your office! Would that be a "second-best" option? Someone who has made an enormous impact despite her limitations from quadriplegia is Joni Eareckson Tada. As she has been willing to "press the limits," her boundaries have turned into blessings. Her painting, writing, and speaking have inspired countless thousands.

How Do I Discover My Own Wiring?

Without question there are many other facets of your wiring that aren't listed here. The point is, however, that you are a unique, priceless, one-of-a-kind individual. You have been wired in a precise and distinct way to find your fulfillment. But to be successful, you need to discover how you are wired.

How do you discover this? Is there a test you can take, a seminar which can bring it all together for you?

Certainly there are many books and tests and seminars along the way which could be helpful. Most Christian bookstores have shelves filled with such materials. For instance, you might read a book such as *Unlocking Your Sixth Suitcase* by John Bradley and Jay Carty.[6] This book helps you think through some of the specifics mentioned in this chapter, but centers on discovering the talents God has built into your life.

Another helpful book is *The Truth About You* by Arthur F. Miller and Ralph T. Mattson.[7] While it is a bit more technical, it does present a practical and insightful approach to getting a handle on who God has created you to be. Rather than using multiple-choice questionnaires, Miller and Mattson ask their readers to use narrative to thoroughly describe who they have been across the course of their lives. Obviously this could never be reduced to a standardized test because each of us is so different. That's why such a process can enormously assist those who are serious about finding their particular slot in life.

A variety of self tests have been developed to help you determine everything from your personality type to your spiritual gifting. Used in concert, these can be most helpful indicators of direction. Some churches even have classes to try to enable this process. Known by a wide variety of names, these classes often include a discussion with a "consultant" in the church who has been trained to help the inquirer discover who God has created them to be.

You Are the Best Judge of You

In the end, however, you are the best judge of you—that is, you and the Lord together. Paul never had the benefit of going through a class, taking a test, or attending a seminar to find out how God had wired him. But as he sought God about his future, as he considered everything he had been through in his life and analyzed his own peculiar gifts and abilities, and as he listened to God, he put everything he had and was to work for the Lord and found the fulfillment that had been designed just for him. The same could be said for Stephen or Timothy or James or a host of other people presented in the New Testament.

The point is, any or all of these approaches can be helpful in discovering how God has built you. You could begin the process of discovery by asking yourself some simple questions:

- What do I do whether I am paid to or not?
- What do I end up doing whether I'm asked to or not, whether anyone else cares or not?
- What do I like to do?
- What am I good at?
- What do people continually see in me?
- What is it that God seems to bless?
- What has God suited me for, designed me to do?
- Where does He appear to be leading me?
- How has God uniquely fashioned me?
- What is God calling me to be? to do?

Once you discover how you are wired, you will find your life journey exploding with excitement and fulfillment. As pieces of the puzzle slip into place, confidence and joy will begin to characterize your life and service. Your lot in life may not be easy, but at least you will know you are headed in the right direction! Don't strive. Simply settle into that special zone that God has designed just for you.

Discover how you are wired!

The Witness

John Prince was wired to win, and he won. But if you had known him as a young sailor during World War II, you never would have imagined what a winner he would be.

A variety of traditions greeted Navy recruits at that time. When the young men arrived fresh from training, the older recruits, who now saw themselves as "old hands," would meet the newer ones at the gangway. They would greet them, gather them in, take them to a local bar, and get them hopelessly drunk. They were in the Navy now, and the new life brought with it new experiences. That's just the way it was!

It was during this time that Dawson Trotman founded the Navigators, a ministry designed to present Christ to servicemen like John. In those early years the ministry had not yet taken on its final form, and the small nucleus of which it was comprised often talked about ways they could minister. As they discussed various Navy traditions, a creative, new plan emerged.

What if, instead of meeting the older recruits at the gangway, the new recruits were welcomed by Christian sailors? And what if those same greeters invited the new recruits to come with them to Dawson's house for a little get-together? Wouldn't that be a great way to get to know them, and perhaps to introduce them to Christ?

It seemed like a workable idea, so they immediately began to put it into practice. Dawson would get his house ready while the other men would go to the gangway, greet the new recruits, and bring home as many as would come to the house.

On one such sortie, a Navigator met John Prince. He immediately felt sorry for the poor fellow because he seemed so out-of-place. He appeared fresh out of the hills, and you couldn't help but wonder whether the Navy had to put shoes on him before they took him in. It was quickly apparent that he didn't have a great deal of formal training, and he may have been limited in other ways as well. But he seemed to warm up to the idea of meeting new friends, so off they went to the preplanned rendezvous.

When they arrived, a number of other fellows were already there. Dawson was doing what he was uniquely gifted to do: milling about, focusing especially on the new recruits. When he came to John, he was taken aback. Why had he been invited? Certainly he wasn't leadership material. With so few Navigators to meet the needs of a huge Navy, they didn't have the extra time it would take for a "project" like John. No, he really didn't fit!

Dawson took aside the Navigator who had invited John and soon received something he was absolutely unprepared for: a rebuke! His young leader pointed out that Jesus had commanded them to preach the gospel to everybody, and John fit that category. Furthermore, he said their group was called merely to sow seed, that it was God's business to do the sorting out. With a large gulp, Dawson apologized and backed off.

Although John was not a Christian, he immediately fit right in. It was as if he had been there all along. He sort of slipped off his shoes and snugged right in. Whenever they had an activity, John could be counted on to be there. He had found his home away from home.

One night a friend of Dawson's named Irwin Moon came to the house and gave a talk. He had developed a fascinating set of presentations using all sorts of electrical paraphernalia, something he called "Sermons from Science." Much later, Moody Bible Institute developed these into a film series that has been used effectively all over the United States. For now, however, it was just Irwin Moon and all his gear in Dawson's house giving a talk to a bunch of interested Navy recruits. His presentation was so intriguing, a guy couldn't help but be provoked by it. At the end of his talk, Irwin gave the men an opportunity to accept Christ.

Irwin's challenge was direct and to-the-point. He simply said that if anyone wanted to accept Jesus Christ as his Savior, he needed to stand up on the spot and say out loud: "I hereby accept Jesus Christ as my Savior!" When he gave that challenge, in a most natural response John Prince leaped to his feet. "I hereby accept Jesus Christ as my Savior!" he proclaimed with no regard for whoever was listening. And with that he entered into a personal relationship with God.

In John's case there was no mistaking the commitment he had made; immediately everything in his life began to change. He was completely caught up in a life with Christ, with Christ as the center of everything.

Like a dry sponge taking in water, John took in every bit of information about Christ he could find. Whenever he had one spare minute, he plunged himself into the Bible. He committed Scripture to memory, a distinct emphasis of the Navigators. Memorization didn't come easy for John, but he knew how important it was and couldn't seem to get enough. The more of the Bible he got, the more he wanted.

More than anything else, John became a witness for Christ. He loved to tell anyone, everyone, anywhere, everywhere about who Jesus Christ was and what He could do in a life. John wasn't shy about sharing his faith. He never seemed to be overly concerned about what he didn't know because he was excited about what he _did_ know. Whatever educational or intellectual gifting he may have lacked was beside the point. He put whatever he had to work for God. He trusted God to use him. Since God delights in willing vessels, John found himself a frontline sailor in God's Navy.

To watch what God did next was nothing short of amazing. John had an uncanny ability to hear and follow God. Could it have been his simple faith? Jesus did say something about how important it is to have faith like that of a little child, and that certainly described John's approach.

On one occasion when he was sitting around with his buddies, John suddenly announced that God wanted him to be the chaplain's yeoman. He somehow knew this was God's desire for that point in his life.

To the other fellows this made no sense. After all, the chaplain's yeoman had to be able to type, write a good letter, and handle both spelling and grammar with some degree of finesse. That certainly didn't describe John! It was wonderful that he had such an intense desire to serve God, but this wasn't even a remote possibility. Oh, they were nice to him. They responded to his remarks with vague affirmation and even wished him well. They just knew it would never happen.

As they were kicking this around, John excused himself for a moment. Less than ten minutes later he returned with glee and announced that he now *was* the chaplain's yeoman! He had gone into the chaplain's office, told him his feelings, and was "hired" on the spot.

How could this have happened? Could it have been that God really did want him there? Could He have made a way where there was no way? The chaplain clearly saw something in John that the others hadn't seen and was willing to take a risk. His openness and freshness to talk about his faith in Christ was extraordinarily winsome. He really was quite a witness!

Whenever John had the opportunity he talked to others about faith in Christ. He also made sure that he had a good supply of simple tracts to leave in their hands. That way they might be able to remember what he had told them and make a commitment whether he was there or not.

When parents of servicemen learned about the ministry of the Navigators, they began to write letters from all over the country asking the Navigators to find their sons and tell them about Christ. It was exceedingly difficult to follow up on those requests because the Navigators themselves never knew which ship was going to be where, or when it was going to be there. More than that, they didn't know for certain if these sailors would still be on the same ship.

Such was the case for John when he ended up with the names of two sailors and the ship they were supposed to be on. Since he didn't know how he would ever meet these fellows, John committed it to God in prayer. Then he climbed aboard a little transport that was taking men out to the ship in question. Of all things, on that trip he managed to sit right next to one of the fellows he was hoping to find!

Unable to locate the other sailor aboard ship, he reboarded the transport to return to shore . . . and who should he find himself seated next to but the other sailor! Coincidence? I don't think so.

John's simple faith and walk with God became so powerful that it became an inspiration for others in the Navigators. From time to time they were reminded of the description in Acts 5 which says that the work done through the apostles was so great that some people were almost afraid to join them. Of course, John himself didn't see it that way. He wouldn't take credit for anything. He saw everything that happened to him as a function of simple faith in Christ.

John eventually got the impression God wanted him to begin a new work, that he was finished with his work on his present ship. Besides, he heard that there was another ship which lacked any sort of strong Christian presence. More importantly, the one Christian who was stationed on that ship had fallen away from Christ and was proving detrimental to the cause. So John announced to his friends that God had called him to change to that ship.

Now transferring ships wasn't that easy. While men did get transferred, there had to be good reason. But that didn't dampen John's resolve. He was on a mission for the King!

So what happened? You guessed it: For no apparent reason, John was transferred to the very ship he felt God was calling him to. He knew that he had his work cut out for him and that he was not up to the task on his own. So he prayed that God would deal with what he was about to face.

No sooner had John set foot on the ship than he came face-to-face with the man who was so antagonistic to Christ. The man spewed venom in John's face as he brushed by. Without a moment's hesitation, John was moved to pray: "Dear Lord, either get this man straightened out with you, or get rid of him!"

That very night this sailor went ashore, got rip-roaring drunk, fell out of a second-story window, and was killed! (I'll let you figure out the theology of this. I'm just reporting the facts.)

When John's ship sailed through the tropics, he bought, carried, and handed out tracts in the language of each country he was visiting. The fact that he was unable to speak the various languages was no barrier. All he knew to do was to be faithful as a witness for Christ.

On one occasion when his ship was tied up in Panama, John grabbed some tracts, a Christian friend, and plowed right through the busy streets of Panama City. Arriving in front of what appeared to be a nice office building, he dragged his friend in and began to go up and down the halls distributing his Spanish tracts. At one point he walked right into a man's office, totally unannounced, and began to talk about Jesus. As it turned out, the man was the Panamanian equivalent of the U.S. Secretary of State. The man not only listened graciously but was so moved that he began to cry and confessed his need for God!

For John it made no difference whether a man was an elected official, a high-ranking figure in the Navy, or a person sleeping on the street. They all needed a Savior and he had been appointed to tell them where and how they could meet Him. John may not have been an eloquent, high-profile intellectual giant, but one fact is undeniably clear: John Prince was wired to win, and he won!

Delight
in Your Wiring

One myth that Americans cherish is that they can be whatever they want to be and do whatever they want to do. All it takes is determination and hard work. With that, you can't miss. You, too, can be president!

Sounds terrific. Unfortunately, it isn't true.

I don't mean to pop anyone's balloon, but this idea is not true physiologically, psychologically, or spiritually. Precisely because of the unique and particular way in which you have been constructed, there are some things that you will be and some that you won't. Likewise, there are some things you will be able to do and some you won't.

But don't let this demoralize you. Remember this: In the end, the only way for you to find fulfillment, completion, satisfaction, happiness, and joy is not by being *anything*, but by being *something*—that special something you were uniquely wired to be.

Discovering how you are wired is the first step in the process. After making that discovery, next you need to delight in it. After all, God does! He crafted you just as He wanted you to be. And no doubt, just as He said after He created the heavens and the earth, He looks at you and says, "That's good! I like it!" If the God of all creation delights in what He has created in you, shouldn't you follow His lead and delight in your construction as well? As you delight in the way in which God has put you together, as you begin to enjoy who you are and how you have been wired, you take the next step in finding true fulfillment and satisfaction.

Delight in Who You Are

Sadly, all sorts of things get in the way of your ability to delight in how you have been fashioned. And even though you may not be responsible for creating them, you will have to deal with them.

First, there are the unrealistic expectations you may have of yourself. In my own case, as a young person I didn't care much for my fair complexion. I had reddish-brown hair and very fair skin. Like all my friends, as I anticipated summer I liked to imagine myself being transformed into one of the men in a Coppertone ad, rippling muscles turned bronze by the sun, wavy black hair blowing in the breeze.

As soon as summer arrived, however, and I was in the sun for more than a minute, my dreams incinerated. Instead of developing a wonderful Coppertone tan, I got burned to a crisp. My color could not be described as "golden brown"; much closer to the truth would be "hot pink," "flamingo," or "neon fuchsia." I kept the local grocery store in business with my purchases of Nivea cream to soothe the pain and itching of my skin. How I longed to look different!

One day when I was about 12, a thought crossed my mind. Why not just become that which I desired to be? Why not wish my reality into existence? With brand-new resolve I imme-diately rode my bicycle to the Capital Shopping Center and entered a local variety store that carried a little bit of every-thing. At the time "big name buttons" were popular with kids my age. These huge accessories featured your name and were to be worn on your coat, shirt, or hat. I walked directly to the counter with those buttons and found exactly the one I needed, the button I would wear, the button with my new name and identity: Tony! That sounded about as Italian as I could imagine, and every Italian I knew had terrific-looking skin and hair. So why not become one of them? Who knows? I might even have a chance with Annette Funicello, the heartthrob of every guy my age!

Funny . . . that button didn't do anything. I still burned to a crisp. My freckles continued to cover my face like a dot-to-dot picture. And my hair never got one bit darker. I finally had to accept that I would continue to look pretty much the way I was created.

As I grew, my looks were hardly the only thing I desired to change. The moment I became a Christian at age 17, for example, I knew I would become a pastor. There was no question in my mind. However God gave me that knowledge, I knew that was what I would do with my life. It was where God wanted me to be, what I was built for. That remained foremost in my mind as I went through college and seminary.

At various junctures along my path, however, I questioned my decision. If I became a lawyer as I thought I would in high school, I could make a great deal more money. I wouldn't have to work weekends, and I would not be on call 24 hours a day. Why not go to law school? Or how about graduate school in psychology? I was a senior scholar in the psychology department of my university and had professors in the department encouraging me to enter a doctoral program at their respective alma maters. Why not do that? Again, it would be challenging, and at the same time not nearly as demanding as pastoring a church. I would have a lot more time to call my own and more freedom to pursue whatever interests I might develop.

Whenever it got down to crunch time, however, I reverted to what I knew I was to do with my life: be a pastor. That decision carried me right through seminary and into the first church I served. And it was an experience in serving that church that helped me get a handle on delighting in the way I was wired.

As you might imagine, pastoring a small, struggling church is a far cry from ministry in an academic setting. In seminary we talked about theology and the critical issues of the day. In the church, people were more interested in who was going to cut the grass around the sign, how we were going to come up with the money for next month's mortgage payment, and whom we could find to run the nursery.

I was totally unprepared for my new situation. In fact, my unmet expectations were so great that after three months I decided to bag the ministry and go to law school. Oh, I would finish out the year. I had committed to that. But as soon as my time was up there were much more exciting, challenging, and fulfilling ways for me to invest my time. Besides, whenever I watched "The Young Lawyers" on television, it appeared as though they were involved in the *real* issues of the day. That was for me!

With that in mind I took the tests, filled out the applications, and received my admittance to law school. Sure, that may not have been what I had geared the last nine years of my life for. But I was still young. Why not go for it while I had the opportunity?

As I neared the end of that first year of pastoring, a chain of events culminated in my being offered a position in management and business ethics at a state university located in the town in which I was living. Since I had done some work in those areas in graduate school, and since it would mean not having to do another graduate degree, it seemed like the right move. I accepted the position and began to make the necessary preparations for switching careers.

Somehow, however, I also committed to continue pastoring the church where I was, except now as a part-timer without pay! I didn't want to let go of pastoring completely and thought the church was small enough that, as long as some of the members moved up a notch in their commitment and involvement, we could do some interesting things.

The moment I began to move my books into my new office on campus, however, everything felt wrong. Outwardly, there was no reason not to rejoice. I had a much better income, worked far shorter hours, and had weekends off. How could you beat that? Besides, Betty and I had purchased a lovely home and no longer had to deal with a parsonage committee. That alone should have brought me contentment. It didn't. Neither did my title of "assistant professor." Other folks in the department took years to get to that position, and here I was beginning there. No question, I should have been ecstatic. But I wasn't.

I began my classes and was having lots of fun. Veterans from the Vietnam War were already filtering back into civilian life, and it seemed as though huge waves of them were crashing on the beach of the business department of my university. Since they were more settled in their lives than students straight out of high school, and often with families, it made for stronger classes. They loved that I was an iconoclast in the business department, and I loved to get them thinking about things few others wanted to touch, such as the social responsibility of business. It was definitely a different environment from my little church filled with people quibbling about lawn mowing.

There was only one problem: It was in that little church that God had designed me to be. And I knew it. It made zero difference how "great" things appeared outwardly; inwardly I was not in the right place, doing the right thing, functioning in accordance with the way I was wired. Ultimately that knowledge led me to give up my teaching position and go back into another small church as pastor. Only this time they didn't quibble about the lawn. They didn't have one. Now the concern was graveling the parking lot! And I was right in the middle of the debate.

But something was different. Now the problem didn't frustrate me so much because I had come to accept that this is where I belonged. I found firsthand the truth that Paul expressed in 1 Corinthians 9:16: "Woe is me if I do not preach the gospel!"

Pastoring is what I was wired to do, and it's where I would find my contentment, peace, and fulfillment. Unrealistic expectations of myself almost kept me from experiencing the joy of being exactly where I was designed to be. And they can keep you from the same thing.

Beware of Others' Expectations

A second roadblock to experiencing fulfillment in who you are is the unrealistic expectations of other people. Indeed, this problem may be far worse than the first.

A wonderful story in the Bible tells about an incident in King David's life when he was just a youth. David was asked by his father to take some food to his brothers who were at a battlefield. On his arrival, David was stunned to find a foreigner mocking not only God's people, but God Himself. Never mind that the one doing the taunting was a giant of a man named Goliath. He had no right to his gibes, and David could not imagine why God's people were shrinking back from engaging him in battle.

Finally, when he could stand it no longer, David volunteered to take on the giant. Though his brothers thought he was crazy and though it made no sense, he still approached King Saul and volunteered his services. Even the good king found the idea outrageous. Did this boy really have what it took to fight the giant? With Israel's future on the line, would David honestly be the best representative they could field?

When David realized that everyone thought his proposal was sheer lunacy, he regaled them with stories in which he had killed bears and lions single-handedly. No matter how great and how strong this giant of a man might be, surely he was no match for wild beasts!

Saul admired the pluck of the young man and allowed him to go head-on-head with Goliath. But before David went, Saul had the young boy clothed in the king's personal armor. His bronze helmet was placed on David's head and the king's coat of mail covered David's body. These pieces of armor had served the king well and they should do the same for David.

As quickly as he had put them on, however, David took them off. They were so heavy that he couldn't even walk. Instead of being a help, they would be a hindrance. While David certainly appreciated the gesture, he assured the king that he would have to fight in his own way, dressed in the manner to which he was accustomed.

En route to engage the giant in battle, David stooped to gather a few stones for the pouch of his sling. They were exactly the kind he liked to use with this weapon he had learned to use so skillfully while guarding his father's sheep. As he approached Goliath, David quickly slipped a smooth stone into the pouch of his sling, swung it rapidly around his head, and let the stone fly. As usual it went right for the target, landing precisely in the middle of Goliath's head, knocking him out and off his feet. Moving in for the kill, David snatched up Goliath's own sword and cut off the giant's head. And thus began the adventures of the greatest of Israel's kings.

Notice that David didn't try to live up to someone else's expectations of how he was to function. If he had tried to, it would have killed him. But because he was willing to stick to his own wiring, he enjoyed great success. Indeed, so did God's people!

The problem of trying to live up to another person's expectations can be frustrating, if not downright devastating. That was brought home to me forcefully in my own ministry.

A beloved member of our church had died and all of us wanted to put together a joyful memorial service. We knew just what to do, partly because before she died I had the opportunity to talk with her about some of her wishes.

The service was truly a celebration of a life lived for the Lord. We laughed together about what a joy she had been and were struck afresh with what a comfort and support and encouragement she had been in a variety of ways to all of us. Truly, her funeral was a wonderful thing. Instead of feeling down in the dumps, everyone was buoyed up. Upon reviewing the life of our friend, we realized that by throwing ourselves headlong into a life in Christ, we too could have rich, full, and meaningful lives.

A week or so later one of our management staff received a letter from someone who had attended the service. While it was addressed to the staff member, it was clear the letter was intended for all four of us on the management team. Reading between the lines, it was first directed at me, and secondarily at the others on the team. The first paragraph was highly complimentary. He reckoned that the service was well-done, and that my message was quite powerful "as usual."

By the second paragraph, however, he began cutting us into strips for everything we had not done. In his opinion, each one of us should have visited this woman in her home at least once a week for the duration of her illness. Secondly, we should have extended that same sort of ministry to her extended family, none of whom attended our church. And thirdly, we really had no compassion for anybody anyway, and probably spent all our spare time huddled in the front of the sanctuary making snide remarks about people in the church, counting the offerings, and designing our next building. Pretty remarkable conclusions for someone who wasn't even part of our church!

Amazingly, smoke didn't roll out of the flap of the envelope, nor was the paper singed. But if ever words on paper were intended to cut into little pieces those who read them, this letter was designed to do just that.

Such a letter would cause many pastors to put a gun to their heads, figuratively if not literally. They would feel overwhelmed that they had let somebody down, that they had neglected to call on this lady as much as they should have, snubbed the extended family, failed to do every last possible thing to cover all bases. They would have beaten themselves up with how miserably they had performed and called into question why they were in ministry in the first place. Slobs that they were, why should they presume to be useful to the Lord and His work?

Pastors sometimes feel this way, and even leave their calling because of it—because they don't match someone's expectations of what they are supposed to be, because they don't do what somebody else thought they were supposed to do. They allow others to afflict them with false expectations for their lives.

I didn't bother to answer the letter. It was obvious this fellow had no interest in hearing what needed to be said. Had I replied, however, I would have noted three things.

First, I would have thanked him for his unintended compliment. While neither I nor my management team had visited this wonderful lady's house every week, people from our church were in her home almost *daily*. As they were scheduled and allowed they visited her, prayed with her, read Scripture to her, made meals for her and her family (yes, even relatives who were visiting), supported her across her difficult days in prayer and presence, and helped out anyplace else they could. In short, the body of Christ was being the body of Christ. The pastors weren't the body, but only a part of it. And if what Paul says is true, that the pastor's role is primarily to equip the saints for the work of ministry, then our people had done their jobs! The church was alive and well, regardless of what our cynical friend thought.

Second, I would have pointed out that the service had gone so well because that is what I was wired to do. I was not wired in the manner of the woman whose life we celebrated; neither was she wired to do what I did. In fact it was only as each of us did that special thing we were individually created to do that we could be all we were meant to be, and the body of Christ could be exactly that—a body, not just a giant heart, finger, or elbow.

Third, I would have offered my hope that the fellow who had written the letter was in a church where his pastor was wired in a way that met this fellow's expectations. If not, both of them were due to be horribly frustrated. The pastor would never be able to live up to this critic's expectations and could never be encouraged to do anything differently. Either way, it would be a lose-lose proposition.

The letter had completely missed the point. Yet how it typifies one of the most common problems we face: trying to live up to the false expectations of other people. The more we try to be what we were never designed to be—regardless of whether the push comes from Aunt Ollie, Professor Johnson, or good old Pastor Friesen—the less fulfilling our lives will be.

Delight in what God has done, not in what other people think ought to happen!

Realize Your Options Aren't Unlimited

A third hindrance to our delighting in the way we've been wired is the assumption that we can become whatever it is we select. All we need to do is put our shoulders to the task and we can make virtually anything happen! Or so we think. Nothing could be further from the truth.

What I am about to say is bound to offend the sensibilities of some. But it is true nonetheless. When Jesus told the parable of the talents (Matthew 25:14-30), He implicitly presented a truth about humanity. Namely, some people are five-talent people, some are two-talent people, and others are one-talent people. The one who has one talent is never going to have two, no matter how hard he tries, nor is the one who has two going to acquire five.

While that may come as bad news to you, the good news is this: God isn't impressed by the number of talents you possess. Rather, His concern is what you do with what you have. Thus, if you are a one-talent person, you need to develop that one talent to its fullest potential. The same is true for two or five. As Jesus says in Luke 12:48: "For everyone to whom much is given, from him much will be required." The idea isn't that if you have one talent, you better work to gain five. It is rather that if you have five, you need to use them all for the glory of God! The same is true if you have one or two.

Lots of frustration develops when folks either try on their own or are encouraged to try that which for them is impossible. Who hasn't heard of pastors desperately striving to preach like Chuck Swindoll, when they simply don't have the basic equipment, the specific talents and giftedness to do so? Or you find someone who enjoys basketball giving everything he has to become Michael Jordan, when the fact is he will be lucky to be chosen when the team captains call out names in his local YMCA. Or how about the lady who is certain she is destined to take Sandi Patti's place, when in reality she sometimes lucks out and actually hits a note that a piano could recognize? No matter how good her backup track, let's face it: It ain't going to happen!

But is that bad? Is it wrong that some people are equipped to do what I can't, or are called to be something I would like to be but haven't been designed for? Is that really so different than my being frustrated with my reddish-brown hair and light complexion, when I would rather appear Southern European?

Just as in the parable of the talents, the point is to be faithful with whatever we are given. If you are a one-talent person, don't worry that you aren't a "two" or a "five." Rather, develop your talent to its fullest potential. It is only when you do, truly delighting in who you are and what you have, that you will ever find that fulfillment you are looking for.

I think Paul had something like this in mind when he wrote in 1 Corinthians 4:7 (NIV),

> For who makes you different from anyone else? What do you have that you did not receive? And if you did receive it, why do you boast as though you did not?

Pastor/author Max Lucado, whom I suspect is a five-talent type, once dealt with this issue in an interview. In response to the question, "Have you ever felt a tension between being faithful to God and faithful to your congregation?" he responded like this:

> Not really, and here's the reason why. For the initial interview, I went through an extra exercise with the elders to clarify whether this was my place. I came up with 15 different expectations people have of a pastor: preaching, study, hospital visitation, administration, and so on, and wrote them on 15 different cards.
>
> I handed a set of 15 cards to each elder and said, "Rank these responsibilities according to what you think are the most important." When everything was tallied, the top three duties, though in different order, were the same for each elder: study, preach,

and teach. When I came here, the elders gave me a one-word job description: message.

I knew what they wanted out of me, and I knew what I could offer. That's a large part of why I accepted the position. Undefined priorities are at the root of much of our success-or-failure frustration.

I told the whole church, "I'm not a counselor or an administrator. I can't keep my own checkbook balanced. I think I'm a decent preacher, and I pledge to you that I will bring the best sermon possible every Sunday. If you complain that so-and-so wasn't visited, I won't feel bad because that's not my main job. But if you say, 'We're not getting good preaching,' I'm going to work on that."[1]

Why is Max winning? Because he is a five-talent person? No. That's beside the point. It's because he has discovered how he is wired and has come to delight in it. And that makes all the difference in the world.

Like Max, God has wired you to win. But if you are ever going to experience the thrill of victory, you need to delight in the way He put you together—even if you do get a sunburn!

The Servant

I f it's possible to discover how you are wired by age five, Patty Stephens did. When she arrived at kindergarten on the first day, Patty noticed a frightened little girl slinking into class who seemed totally intimidated by the whole experience. But instead of sharing her fright, Patty took her by the hand and offered to spend the day with her. That simple action set the pace for the rest of her life.

By age ten, Patty got up before everyone in the family except her dad. After making breakfast for her brother and sister, she would quietly call them to breakfast. She didn't want them to get up on the wrong side of the bed, nor did she want to wake her mom. After all, Mom had lots of work to do and needed a few extra winks! When Patty got home after school, she baked a Betty Crocker cake almost every afternoon, set up the ironing board and did ironing for the family as she talked with her mom who was working on a home-based business. You better believe that Patty was wired to serve, because that was the hallmark of her entire life.

Growing up in a church family, it seemed as though she always had a tender heart for God. But it was when a good friend died in an accident in the seventh grade that she really cemented her relationship with the Lord. As she grew, she suffered through many tests and trials, but her faith continued to develop and become ever deeper and richer. It came to be the centerpiece of her existence, the foundation for everything. Over time she came to understand that as she served, she was really showing her love to the Lord and the Lord's love to other people. That thought motivated her to serve even more. Patty was totally sold-out to God, and desired to bless Him with every aspect of her life.

She married and started a family at a younger age than most of her peers. Instead of seeing that as a problem, however, she threw herself completely into it. She was devoted to her husband and to her two boys. As they grew, though she sometimes rebuked and exhorted them to their faces, behind their backs she was their greatest defender. After all, God had given her this family. And she loved them dearly!

Patty was so devoted to her family that when she and her husband built a new house, they designed it with aging parents in mind. More than that, they built it to house every possible extended family function. That way, everybody would always have someplace to go. Because of that arrangement, she was able to become the primary care-giver for the last five years of her grandma's life. She counted it a blessing to be able to serve in this way. Of course, there were the usual hassles that go with other people moving in with your family, but so what? She got to serve. And that's what she was designed for.

This remarkable woman was so motivated to serve and encourage others that she found it hard to take no for an answer. One time she planned a ski outing to the mountains with her family. It would be a great, relaxing weekend for them all. When the appointed time arrived, however, there was virtually no snow. How could this be? She had planned for them to take a sleigh ride. How dare it not snow!

Mother Nature should have known better. Such a snub could never deter a woman like Patty. If a sleigh ride she had planned, a sleigh ride they would take. Somehow Patty managed to talk the owner of the sleigh (as well as an unbelieving family!) into taking that ride, and off they rode in a cloud of dust, sparks flying from the runners.

Shortly before her grandma died, Patty had planned a large extended-family gathering at the coast. When she talked with Grandma about it, Grandma wanted no part of it. It would take too long to drive there. It would be too much trouble to take her. The weather might not cooperate. It seemed as if Grandma had a reason it wouldn't work for every possible benefit Patty presented. But Patty held her ground. Grandma was going; that's all there was to it. Patty would serve her grandma whether she liked it or not!

Evidently Patty had inherited her stubborn streak from Grandma, because a couple of days before the trip, Grandma died. Now she wouldn't have to go! It looked as if Grandma would get the last laugh. Or would she? As they were preparing for the funeral, Patty got a special gleam in her eye, smiled a smile that became almost a trademark for her, and exclaimed to her family, "You know, we *still* could take Grandma!"

Everyone knew, of course, that this would never happen, but it reminded the whole family of Patty's tenacity to serve. If there were any avenue of service open to her, Patty would find it. It just so happened that this time Grandma had chosen a route which Patty could not follow.

Don't think for a moment that Patty reserved her servant heart for her family. She expressed it to anyone. In her church, for example, she threw herself into "The Great Escape," the annual high-school summer retreat. She didn't fill the role of someone "front and center." Rather, she became part of the cooking crew. How much more of a servant can you get?

Every day she was one of the first ones up and one of the last ones to go to bed. She was always the first one in the kitchen and greeted the other cooks with a hearty rendition of the "Hallelujah Chorus" as they dragged in to start their day. As they glared at her as if to say, "When did they release you?" she would announce that they were all going to paint their faces green and greet the campers as Martians. Or maybe they would wear party hats and fake noses. Certainly they wanted to perk up these kids!

As soon as the cooking was done, you would find Patty counseling or praying with one of the girls at the camp. Always sensitive to those who were hurting, she zeroed in on them immediately and gave of her time unhesitatingly. She loved to serve and served to love.

When she developed a brain tumor at age 43 and found that she had a limited time to live, Patty was much more concerned about how other people would feel than about herself. She didn't want to put anybody out who might feel obligated to serve her, and often cheered up those who came to encourage her! Still, because she had been such a loving, giving, caring person through her life, all sorts of people reached out to help her during that last year. Whereas she had been so busy serving during her lifetime that she never had time to be served herself, now it was time to receive that which she had given.

Right to the end, Patty was a servant. That's how she was created. That's where she found her fulfillment. And that is what gave her life its zip. Whether it was in changing a catheter for the elderly man down the street whose wife was blind, taking cookies to someone who had just returned from the hospital, or making meals for a friend who was going through a bout of depression, Patty served. That's how she was wired.

At her memorial service, hundreds gathered to celebrate her life. Odd . . . she was "just a housewife." They aren't supposed to make that kind of impact, are they? Yet the simple truth is that she made a dent deeper than the Grand Canyon on all those her life touched. Why? Because she knew how she was wired, she delighted in it, and she gave herself away for Jesus Christ.

Patty didn't run the race to finish; she ran to win. You know what? She did!

Why Everyone Can Win

Everybody wants to win. You can see it most any Saturday morning on the soccer fields and softball diamonds throughout the land. As the kids play their hearts out trying to win the game, their parents lose their voices cheering them on. In more cases than you might think, the victory means more to the parents than it does to the children. That's why they threaten, cajole, curse, and badger their little ones to hustle more, run faster, throw harder, and sacrifice their little bodies to score.

If you live in a state which has a lottery, you can see this same desire to win most any Saturday afternoon in the corner convenience store. Though these people would be honking their horns frantically if someone ahead of them hesitated just a few moments when a traffic light turned green, they'll stand in line for hours just to get their precious lottery tickets. Who knows? Maybe they'll buy the winning ticket!

Time and again at mailboxes all over the country, men and women anxiously watch for the postman, hoping their entries in the Publisher's Clearing House giveaway will be their ticket to the easy life. Sure, there may be a greater chance that they will be struck by lightning than win the contest, but doesn't somebody have to win? Why not them? Why not this time?

The same quest is obvious as people plunge whatever time and money they have into the newest get-rich-quick scheme. They've seen sure bets come and go more times than they would like to remember, but *this* one is going to be different. This time the products really are so good and the prices so low that they can't lose! As they excitedly slap photos of that dream home on their refrigerator, as they shove the most recent motivational cassette into the recorder to get revved up, there's no doubt about it. They're going to win!

Hour after hour on television channels you can see this same desire inflamed by the "infomercials." It all looks so good, seems so easy. All it takes is getting your brain supercharged, your body superslimmed, your bank account superfilled. And if you would just send $149.95 to the address listed on the screen or phone the 800 number and put it on your VISA, there's just no question: You'll be a winner!

Everybody wants to win. Everybody wants to be happy. Everyone pursues satisfaction, contentment, a sense of meaning and purpose—albeit unintentionally. They all want a life that is successful, fulfilled, and free from pain and problems.

What Does It Really Mean to Win?

When I first met Henry, he certainly seemed to be a winner. At least that's how he looked to me. I was a young and inexperienced pastor, over my head in my first large building project. The real costs of our new church facility were exceeding our anticipated costs significantly, and we needed additional capital to finish. So we did the obvious thing: We returned to the bank that initially loaned us the money to build and asked them to increase the loan.

As I took a seat in the sumptuous corporate office of my banker, I thought I could vaguely hear the strains of, "You must pay the rent, you must pay the rent!" My lips were beginning to form around the usual words, "I can't pay the rent, I can't pay the rent," when I was shaken back to reality by the lender who was saying, "Sorry. No can do!" With his gesture that indicated the meeting was over and I was now supposed to disappear out the door, I crept out.

After countless sleepless nights and prayerful days, I finally found out about Henry and landed in his office. He was a money broker and appeared to be able to figure out a way to meet our needs and do what our own bank so emphatically had refused to do.

I felt as though I had ascended into the heavens just to get to Henry's office, located on the zillionth floor of a very classy office building in downtown Portland, just across the river from my home in Vancouver. As I emerged from the elevator and sank into the carpet, I realized that his firm took up one whole side of the floor. Two huge mahogany doors stood between me and my appointment, and after taking a good look, I wanted to catch the next elevator back to planet Earth. Man, was I out of my element. Summoning up all my courage, however, I pressed on. What did I have to lose?

After introducing myself to the receptionist, I was quickly and cordially ushered into Henry's office. What an office it was! From his desk, Henry overlooked most of the city of Portland and the Willamette River as well. It was breathtaking, and none of it was lost on me. Henry quite obviously was "in the chips," making big deals and getting commensurately big commissions.

As he rose from behind his massive desk, I realized his suit probably cost more than my car. He was dressed impeccably, from the soles of his Allen Edmonds to the collar of his Armani. Even his cuff links dazzled my pastoral eyes as he stretched out his hand to shake my own. And then we both sat down to talk business.

Talk about being out of my league! To get us on more common ground, I asked him some questions of a personal nature. How long had he lived in Portland? How was his business doing? How did he like what he did? How would he like to tithe to my church? (I didn't really ask him that last one, but I wanted to!)

As he talked about himself, he seemed to relax. Maybe it was because he was on solid ground. Maybe because he liked to brag a little. Maybe because he liked me and saw that I was no threat. Whatever the reason, Henry got on a roll.

Over the course of the next few minutes he let me know that he was truly a winner. There was no need for him to tell me—everything from his suit to his surroundings shouted his status. He informed me that downstairs in the parking garage, in spot number one next to the elevator, he had the largest BMW known to man. Thus he arrived in total comfort, and because he only had to walk about ten feet to the elevator, he remained that way!

He was married, had several kids, a new house, and all the accoutrements that pertained thereto. He had a stereo system that when cranked up could empty a cemetery, and his collection of gadgets defied the imagination.

The more he talked, the more clear it became: This man was a winner. Everything he had and was virtually screamed that here was the embodiment of success—or so I thought until that funny look crossed his face.

I watched as the emptiness swallowed his expression of delight. His appearance became melancholy, downright sad. Looking right at me, he said,

> You want to hear something funny? A couple of nights ago, after everybody in the company had gone home, I sat right here at this desk and thought about my situation. The view here is even more spectacular at night, with all the lights of the city reflecting off the river. I thought about how lucky I was to "have it all," you know, to have the "stuff." People would practically kill for my parking spot, let alone for my car. I have an income greater than anything I ever imagined, and can do pretty much anything I want. I have a wife, and kids, and all the usuals. But you know what? As I thought about myself and my situation, it was everything I could do to stop myself from jumping right through this

> window and ending it all. See, I've got everything.
> But really, I've got nothing! Now that I've got what I
> thought I always needed, I'm no happier than I was
> before I had any of it. I don't get it!

I was dumbfounded. Outwardly, Henry seemed a winner. But once you got below the surface, he looked a whole lot different. Why? Because reaching the American Dream and winning are not synonymous. As a younger man, Henry had already attained what most folks spend a lifetime trying to gain. And yet once he "had it all," he found it meant precious little.

The Ephemeral American Dream

What constitutes the American Dream? The truth is, the whole concept is up for grabs. It usually represents whatever notch of life is at least one up from wherever you happen to be at the moment. If you are now living in 1200 square feet, the 1500-square-foot house across the street is your dream home. (Which is fine, because the people who occupy it are dreaming about moving to the 2000-square-foot home in a much nicer area across town!) If you are making $25,000 a year now, you could live much more comfortably and joyfully on $40,000. And on it goes. The problem is that whenever you reach the next plateau, you're already captivated by the one beyond.

If reaching the American Dream were the same as winning, then Donald Trump would have taken home the prize several years ago. But when he went through bankruptcy and was placed on an "austerity" budget of $465,000 a month, nobody considered him a winner any longer. *Having* is never the same as *winning*.

When you go to the Bible, you find a much richer and fuller understanding of winning. It is developed especially well in the writings of Paul. In 1 Corinthians 9:24-27 (TLB), the apostle lays it all out:

> In a race, everyone runs but only one person gets
> first prize. So run your race to win. To win the

> contest you must deny yourselves many things that would keep you from doing your best. An athlete goes to all this trouble just to win a blue ribbon or a silver cup, but we do it for a heavenly reward that never disappears. So I run straight to the goal with purpose in every step. I fight to win. I'm not just shadow-boxing or playing around.

> Like an athlete I punish my body, treating it roughly, training it to do what it should, not what it wants to. Otherwise I fear that after enlisting others for the race, I myself might be declared unfit and ordered to stand aside.

The word translated as "win" in this passage is a member of an illustrious family of words. It has a broad range of meanings, which combined give a sense of what winning is all about. It means to be complete, fulfilled, satisfied, full-grown, mature, whole, or perfect. It assumes that you are content regardless of your circumstances, joyful in spite of whatever is going on in your life (which explains why Henry was not winning). You have a quiet kind of confidence that somehow everything is going to work out, even though it may not look that way. You have peace, knowing that when everything appears to be out-of-control, you belong to God, who has absolutely everything in control. And that includes your life!

Winning thus means being where you are supposed to be, doing what you have been designed to do, knowing that God is on your side, and feeling good about it. Regardless of the evaluations or expectations of others. Regardless of your physical or financial condition. Regardless of the limitations you might face.

That's why Paul was a winner. We will go into this in greater depth later, but by his own admission he knew how to win with everything or with nothing. He knew how to triumph in the jaws of obvious defeat. Why else do you think he could be beaten, cast into jail, locked in stocks, and still sing hymns of praise to God? Was he a wacko . . . or was he a winner?

As you consider Paul, please notice something else. He was committed to *winning*. He wasn't interested merely in finishing. All too often it seems that folks are happy just to finish. They see winning as frosting on the cake—nice, but not necessary. Paul thought there was an enormous difference between the two. Notice he did not say "run to finish"; he said "run to *win*"!

The last event in the 1992 Summer Olympics was the marathon. As if running 26 miles wasn't enough, the people who designed the course decided it should climax in a two-mile climb that ended in the stadium in front of 40,000 screaming fans. When the runners had reached the summit, they broke onto the track where everyone in the stadium could cheer on their favorites.

As the leader in this particular Olympic marathon entered the stadium and his identity became known, most everyone went wild. A South Korean was in the lead and clearly was going to win. He easily outdistanced his closest competitor, a runner from Japan. The significance of this battle was expressed in the finish of these two. The last time a South Korean had won, Korea was occupied by Japan. The Japanese had forced a Korean to run under a Japanese name, as if he were Japanese. That way, when he won, his medal counted for the Rising Sun. As far as the Korean was concerned, it was the height of humiliation. But not this time—not in 1992.

Shouts could be heard all over Barcelona as the South Korean runner jogged onto the track, straining for the tape. The stadium erupted in wild applause. After breaking through the winner's tape, the runner desired to take the traditional winner's lap, but couldn't. After running so hard for so long, he could only make it about a hundred yards before he collapsed. He was exhausted. But he was also victorious. He had run to win, and he had won!

A few hours later, when the closing ceremonies were well underway in that same stadium, the last runner finally finished the race. Only he didn't get a hero's welcome. In fact, he didn't get a welcome at all. Unlike the winner, he didn't even get to enter the stadium. Instead he was shunted off to a practice track beside the stadium to finish. No cheers. No greeting. No crowd. He had run the same course, conquered the same climb, and finished the race. But that's all. He merely finished. He hadn't won. And that little fact made all the difference.

It's true that when it comes to your faith in Christ, you can finish without exerting yourself too hard. You can confess Christ. You can be assured a place with Him forever in His kingdom.

And you can still not win.

Why? Because while you might rejoice with the Lord forever, you will miss out on the abundance He had for you in this life. Jesus said, "I have come that [you] might have life, and that [you] may have it more abundantly" (John 10:10). You'll also miss out on the rich rewards He longs to lavish on you at the end of the course. You'll make it to heaven, but that's about it. You will be saved, "but only as one escaping through the flames" (1 Corinthians 3:15 NIV).

Jesus didn't come merely to give you an existence. It was His clear intention that you enjoy a certain fullness, a depth of joy and satisfaction and contentment in the very act of living. It is a given that this abundance will exist in heaven. It should be a given that all God's people have a foretaste of it here as well. How can that happen? By running to win, not merely to finish. That's what Paul did with his life, and that is what he sets forth for all those who would follow him.

Want to hear something that may sound strange? God has fashioned you for the same kind of fulfillment enjoyed by Paul. He has made available to you every resource that affords contentment and joy. Even if you have thought yourself to be unworthy or felt you were not good enough to attain such a thing, it's yours for the taking.

The Commercialization of Discontent

Before proceeding any further, let me caution you about something. Society seems to be organized to drive you to discontent!

Discontent fuels the fires of much of the advertising industry. If you are to buy a new car, you have to become discontented with your current one. (For some, that may not take much pressure!) If you are to buy a new pair of sneakers, you have to feel there is something inadequate about the old ones. No one hopes to get you to buy something unless he can entice you to try it. So people work on making you uncomfortable until you do things their way.

Discontent seems to fuel the media in general. Watch the evening news. When was the last time you saw a story which highlighted Suzy Anderson, daughter of Tom and Sarah Anderson, who got straight A's for the tenth straight year? Not only has she never missed a day of class, but she loves to do homework! No, more likely you have been treated to the latest firebombing, racial slur, political gaff, sexual dalliance, health hazard, or environmental crisis. Who wants to hear about the good things? It's greed, gossip, and garbage that grabs our attention.

Society just isn't set up to help you win. It pushes you to seek the quick fix in everything from marital bliss to managerial success. But do any of those quick fixes really work over the long haul? If so, why do we want a whole set of new ones as each year rolls around?

That's precisely why you need to rise above your environment and see the bigger picture. That's why you need to see things from God's point of view. He is the One who designed you, after all. He created you for contentment, wired you to win. As you begin to understand and approach life His way, winning finally becomes more of a reality than a fantasy. You just need to discover the key to how it all works!

The Songwriter and the Preacher

The concept of winning developed in this book is not a new idea. Most of the winners I've chosen to highlight are contemporaries, but that shouldn't imply that God's people have only recently figured out how to win. This chapter will present two winners from the past—one a woman, the other a man; one an American, the other an Englishman; one from the nineteenth century, the other from the eighteenth. But both with one tremendous thing in common: They were wired to win, and they won!

The Songwriter

One of the most prolific hymn writers of all time was Frances Jane "Fanny" Crosby. During her lifetime she wrote almost 9000 hymns, sometimes at the rate of three per week. In the Christian community Fanny Crosby's name is legendary. But it isn't just because of her ability to produce hymns. It is rather because of her single-minded devotion to serve God with her whole being. She was wired to win and won!

Fanny's life was hard from the very beginning. At six weeks of age she was inadvertently blinded when a physician prescribed the wrong treatment for a simple eye infection. What should have been a routine treatment turned into tragedy. Whatever those little eyes were able to take in for six precious weeks would have to serve her for a lifetime, because that is virtually all she would ever see. Fanny would be able to distinguish between night and day and even see vivid colors if placed against the right background. But she would never enjoy the beauty and grandeur of creation that has inspired artists of all kinds. She would never be able to discern the subtlety of color that makes life so breathtaking. She would never see the cascading hues on the wings of a monarch butterfly, never catch a glimpse of a deer prancing across a meadow, never perceive the blush on a person caught up in love.

For some people such a tragedy would create ugly scars which would warp life forever. Bitterness would harden them and compound their handicap. Or they might give in to their limitations and fear to risk the "impossible"—but not Fanny.

Commenting as an adult on her blindness, she said: "The good Lord, in His infinite mercy, by this means consecrated me to the work that I am still permitted to do."[1] In addition, she proclaimed, "Sightless, I see, and, seeing, find soul-vision, though my eyes are blind."[2] Her blindness may have been caused by a physician's blunder, but she considered it a blessing. It helped her focus more fully on the God she was so devoted to serve.

Fanny had a special interest in God, even as a little girl. Although she didn't have what she considered a total conversion experience until she was 30 years of age, as a youngster she had a true hunger for God and His Word. That hunger led her to memorize the entire Pentateuch, most of the Psalms, and all of the books of Proverbs, Ruth, The Song of Solomon, and all four Gospels! That devotion to the Bible became the foundation for the direction God desired to take her in life.

As much as possible, Fanny was a normal child. Like her friends, she rode horses, climbed trees, and joined in the outdoor games everybody else played. Being quite musical, she learned to play the guitar and then added the piano, organ, and harp to her instrumental repertoire.

But what set her apart from other people, even as a little girl, was her knack for poetry. It was as if she were born to write poems. She composed from the time she was eight years old. During her years as both a student and teacher at the Institution for the Blind in New York, she came to be known as the "blind poetess." In fact, one of her first recorded poems dealt with her blindness. At age eight she expressed herself like this:

> Oh, what a happy soul am I!
> Although I cannot see,
> I am resolved that in this world
> Contented I will be.

> How many blessings I enjoy
> That other people don't;
> To weep and sigh because I'm blind,
> I cannot, and I won't.[3]

As her three strengths in poetry, music, and a love for the Word of God were blended, they formed a power that God used to touch the lives of millions.

Fanny's powerful experience with the Lord at age 30 couldn't be called a conversion. She had been a believer throughout most of her life. But she believed her relationship with the Lord was not vital, that she had never yielded herself completely to God. She thus came to the point of feeling something was wrong. There didn't seem to be real depth and energy in her life with the Lord.

Finally she made a decision to "get right" with God, and earnestly sought a new and deeper level of relationship with Him at a series of church meetings. On the last night as she labored at the altar rail in prayer, she suddenly leaped to her feet and shouted, "Hallelujah! Hallelujah!" The encounter with God she had been searching for took place! However you choose to label it, in that moment something powerful transpired.[4] From that point on, she knew her relationship with the Lord had reached a depth she had never experienced.

Little changed outwardly in Fanny's life, but great changes took place within. Her faith was no longer lukewarm; she wanted to live full-throttle for the Lord, giving Him her very best. As she said, "My very soul was flooded with celestial light. For the first time I realized that I had been trying to hold the world in one hand and the Lord in the other."[5] In addition, "The Lord planted a star in my life and no cloud has ever obscured its light."[6] An inner transformation had taken place, and as a result things would never be the same.

Fanny was not merely committed; she was now consumed. She was not just invested; she was now truly addicted to God! Though several years passed before she would put everything she had to work for the Lord, she was clearly headed in that direction and never looked back.

For almost 14 years, Fanny struggled to figure out exactly what she was supposed to be doing for the Lord. Here and there she composed a hymn that was meaningful to her and to other people, but something wasn't right. She didn't have that sense that she was exactly where she was supposed to be, doing what she was supposed to be doing. She wasn't "home" yet. At first this sense was only a minor irritation, but over time she simply couldn't get it out of her mind. Hour after hour, day after day, she felt her insides knot up with anxiety. How could she truly make her life count for the Lord? What was she supposed to be doing?

Some people assume that "God's will for my life" will be easy to figure out. And for some it is. But for the vast majority it isn't. It's all too easy to feel as though God's plan is locked away somewhere, and you don't know where it is locked or how to unlock it! That was the case with Fanny. She knew that she was gifted in poetry, music, and knowledge of the Word, but what was she supposed to do about it?

The only thing she could do was go from church to church, pastor to pastor, and ask people what they thought. She figured that perhaps someone might have the key that would unlock the door to her future. She was relentless, even though it took years for her search to come to an end.

When Fanny was talking one day with a pastor named Peter Stryker, he suggested that she get together with William Bradbury, a man well-known for writing gospel songs. Pastor Stryker knew Bradbury, knew he was looking for someone to help him with his writing, and thought Fanny could be that someone. So he offered to arrange a meeting. Fanny leaped at the chance and told him she would be delighted to get together with Bradbury.

Pay close attention to what happened next. Don't miss a bit of it! It could be the key that unlocks the door to your own future with the Lord, or helps you to unlock the door for another person.

Just knowing that she would be meeting this well-known songwriter, Fanny practically floated home. Maybe this was it! Maybe this was what she had been waiting for all these years! As she got home and ruminated on the forthcoming meeting, she suddenly had a vision. She was no longer in her home. Instead, she was now in heaven. And what transpired while she was there proved monumental for her future. As she described it:

> I was in an immense observatory, and before me was the largest telescope I had ever imagined. I could see everything plainly. . . . Looking in the direction pointed out by my friend, I saw a very bright and captivating star, and was gradually carried toward it—past the other stars, and any amount of celestial scenery that I have not the strength even to describe.
>
> At last we came to a river and paused there. "May I not go on?" I asked of my guide. "Not now, Fanny," was the reply. "You must return to the earth and do your work there, before you enter those sacred bounds; but ere you go on, I will have the gates opened a little way, so you can hear one burst of the celestial music."

> Soon there came clouds of melody such as I never
> had supposed could exist anywhere: the very recol-
> lection of it thrills me.[7]

In this encounter with God, triggered by her expectation of a meeting that lay ahead, Fanny realized what she was to do with her life. In some ways, whether she ever got together with Bradbury was irrelevant. She now knew what direction she would take, exactly where it was that God wanted to use her. From this point on, she would write hymns for the Lord and in them try to capture the "celestial music" she heard in her vision. Just think what it would do for people to be able to sing songs that reflected the Lord in His true glory! If only she could do that, truly she would be "home."

It were as if the Lord had awakened a sleeping giant. Just during the decade of the 1870s, for example, among the hundreds of other songs she wrote were "Safe in the Arms of Jesus," "Blessed Assurance," "Pass Me Not, O Gentle Savior," "Jesus, Keep Me Near the Cross," "I Am Thine, O Lord," "All the Way My Savior Leads Me," "Close to Thee," "Praise Him, Praise Him!" "To God Be the Glory," and "Rescue the Perishing."[8] Most hymn writers would be ecstatic to have written one or two of these. But ten? And that was only a tiny sampling of what she wrote.

Not only did the Lord give Fanny numerous gifts, He also filled her to the brim with boundless energy! In addition to her hymn writing, she also gave herself continually to encouraging men in the Bowery who were down-and-out. She also was called on often to speak, which she enjoyed and did quite well. Even as Fanny got older, her energy never waned. At age 84 she had to have two traveling companions because her pace was just too much for one. They had to switch off just to keep up with her!

How central was the writing of hymns to Fanny's life? That's like asking how important blood is for the heart or oxygen for the lungs. Her hymns were such a part of who she was that it is impossible to understand her life apart from them. Fanny once said that if she were ever forced to stop writing her hymns, she would die within a year! Her work was so much a part of her that it seemed as natural as breathing. To some it may have appeared too easy. But it was what God had designed and divinely appointed her to do.

An event in 1868 illustrates the relative ease with which Fanny approached her work. One day her friend Dr. W.H. Doane rushed into her house and said, "I have exactly 40 minutes before my train leaves for Cincinnati. Here is a melody. Can you write words for it?" Without a moment's hesitation, Fanny replied that she would do whatever she could. "Then followed a space of twenty minutes during which I was wholly unconscious of all else except the work I was doing. At the end of that time I recited the words to 'Safe in the Arms of Jesus.' Mr. Doane copied them, and had time to catch his train."[9] What a unique gifting of God, coupled with a willingness to apply it!

Fanny never saw her writing as a way to be either famous or wealthy. Though she did become well-known, she never made great sums of money. For the most part she never received more than two dollars for any song she ever wrote, and not more than $400 in a given year. But that wasn't the point. Her desire was to use her music to reach people with the grace and life of God, to let them share a moment of heavenly vision. In the early years of her hymn writing, Fanny prayed that the Lord would use her songs to bring a million people to Him. Not bad for someone whom many others would have pitied because of her "handicap"!

Whether a million people actually met Jesus through her songs we may never know. But the number of lives she touched greatly exceeded her goal. Her songs have been sung by peasants in the Alps of Switzerland, by royalty in England, by presidents in the United States of America, and even by Bedouins in the deserts of Arabia![10] In fact, Fanny's songs have continued to reach multitudes of people long after her passing. Although she died in 1915, one of her songs didn't become truly popular until 1954. Somewhere along the line, evangelist Billy Graham had heard one of Fanny's more obscure hymns. He so liked it that he introduced it at a 1954 crusade in

England. Before the crusade ended, people were heard singing or humming it in bus queues, on the underground, and in restaurants. Graham liked the song and the response to it so well that when he returned home he used it in Nashville, Tennessee. Before that crusade was over, "To God Be the Glory," one of Fanny's lesser-known works, was a worldwide favorite—and that 39 years after Fanny's death!

In a biography of Fanny's life, Bernard Ruffin includes a story of an incident that occurred when she was already in her nineties. It is a perfect portrayal of a winner.

The year is 1910. The place is Perth, Amboy, New Jersey. A hackman stops to pick up two passengers. One is a middle-aged clergyman; the other is a withered old crone, apparently blind, ravaged and wasted almost beyond belief, bent nearly double with age. But as the coach jolts along en route to the railroad depot, the hackman becomes aware that there is something unusual about this ancient woman, seemingly straight out of one of Grimms' *Fairy Tales*. She is speaking to the clergyman. Her voice is not dry and quavering, as one might be led from her appearance to expect, but it is clear and high and mellow and young. Far from the senility that one might expect in one so venerable (she must be more than a hundred!), the lady's mind is as fresh and young as her voice. She evidently is a woman of great intellect and refinement. She and the clergyman are discussing some point of theology. The coachman listens intently to the wit and wisdom the old lady displays. When it becomes obvious that the driver is paying more attention to what she is saying than to the road, the minister speaks up.

"This is Fanny Crosby, the hymn writer," he says. The hackman is stunned. He stops his horse, takes off his hat, and weeps openly. Getting himself together, he proceeds to the depot, where he searches for a policeman and finds one. He introduces the old woman to him. "This is Miss Fanny Crosby that wrote 'Safe in the Arms of Jesus.' I want you to help this young man get her safely to the train."

The cop is stunned. "I sure will," he says. Then he says, falteringly, to the little old lady, "We sang your hymn, 'Safe in the Arms of Jesus' last week—at my little girl's funeral."

As he looks at the ground with reddened and shining eyes, "Aunt Fanny" takes his enormous arm in her skinny hands and says, with great feeling and tenderness, "My boy, I call all policemen and railroad men 'my boys,' they take such good care of me wherever I go— God bless your dear heart! You shall have my prayers! And tell your dear wife that your dear little girl is 'Safe in the Arms of Jesus.' "

With these words, the constable broke down and wept openly.[11]

Truly, Fanny Crosby was wired to win and won. Few have had the impact on the world that she has had, and that because she was simply willing to be what God had created her to be and do what God had created her to do. She never lost precious time worrying about her difficulties. Rather, she was so caught up in her opportunities that she wanted every second to count for the kingdom. God does awesome things through fully yielded vessels!

The Preacher

As a young man Charles Simeon had no place for God in his life. He was consumed by his appearance and athletic prowess, and his character was marked by a temper that was often out-of-control. Who would have thought that he would become one of England's most influential clergymen? How unlikely that he would set the pace for biblical preaching and influence the development of preachers and missionaries who would in turn influence believers all over the world! Look with me at the life of this man, and you'll see one who was truly wired to win and won.

Charles Simeon met the Lord in 1779, his first year in college. It happened quite unintentionally. He was not earnestly seeking God, but God was obviously seeking him. Much to Simeon's horror, upon his arrival at school he found that all students were to take part in Holy Communion. Although he was not truly a believer, he was enough of a cultural Christian to know that communing without faith could be dangerous to his health. He knew the apostle Paul warned people not to participate in communion unless they truly understood and were caught up in what was taking place (1 Corinthians 11:28-30). He therefore began to set his spiritual house in order by reading Scripture and examining his own life.

While the communion service itself did not transform Simeon's life, God used it in a powerful way to get the ball rolling. Simeon didn't know it, but he was hooked on God! Just getting ready for that first communion whetted his appetite for a relationship with God, and afterward he couldn't shake the idea that there might be a place for him in God's family. Yet it made no sense to him that God would have a spot for someone as wretched as he.

In the process of reading and preparing himself for the upcoming celebration of Easter, he experienced something that would forever change and mark his life. As he was reading a book about the Lord's Supper, he wrote:

> I met with an expression to this effect, "that the Jews knew what they did when they transferred their sin to the head of their offering." The thought rushed into my mind, "What? May I transfer all my guilt to Another? Has God provided an offering for me that I may lay my sins on his head? Then, God willing, I will not bear them on my soul one moment longer." Accordingly, I sought to lay my sins upon the sacred head of Jesus, and on the Wednesday began to have a hope of mercy; on the Thursday that hope increased; on the Friday and Saturday it became more strong; and on the Sunday morning (Easter Day) I woke early with those words upon my heart and lips "Jesus Christ is risen today! Hallelujah! Hallelujah!" From that hour peace flowed in rich abundance into my soul, and at the Lord's

table in our chapel I had the sweetest access to God
through my blessed Savior.[12]

In that one experience Charles Simeon was hooked on
God, consumed by Christ, and immersed forever in His wonderful grace and love. That would be his theme song from that
moment on. He would never forget the condition he was in
when Christ met, loved, and accepted him. And that humility
became a model for all others who ever sat under the ministry
of this man.

Perhaps because his life was so transparent that you could
see his joy, the first church he pastored began to grow immediately. Within a couple of months a church that had been "dry
as a bone" was so packed out that it looked like "a theater on
the first night of a play."[13] Imagine, a young, inexperienced
preacher seeing what it meant for people to be touched by the
love of God so powerfully that it impacted the whole community! God had taken all of the education, background, talent,
and passion of this young man and fashioned it into an arrow
that would pierce the heart of a nation. God was also giving
him a taste of what was in store for him. He would need it. The
years ahead weren't going to be easy!

Within a year Simeon was transferred to Holy Trinity
Church in Cambridge. It was his dream to pastor this church
someday, but never in his wildest imagination did he guess that
it would happen so quickly. Now he was heir to one of the most
prestigious pulpits in all England.

Given his training, youth, and success, his new assign-
ment seemed destined to continue with the same momentum.
No such luck! Simeon stepped squarely into a church filled
with people disinterested in hearing the Bible taught. As he
began to preach his solidly biblical messages with passion, he
was immediately labeled an "enthusiast." The congregation
viewed him as a wild-eyed radical. Fearful of what he might
bring into the church, they wasted no time in trying to shut him
down. Those who owned locking pews neither showed up in
church, nor unlocked their pews for other people to occupy.
They wanted to make certain they did their part to discourage
attendance, thereby discouraging the preacher.

When Simeon countered by placing benches in the aisles for people to sit on, the wardens of the church pulled the benches outside. Rowdies were hired to come and disturb the services, making it unattractive and difficult for people to attend. Indeed, it was not unusual for Simeon to be "egged" when he left church after Sunday services.

It would have been hard enough had this gone on for a month or two—but for ten years? Nevertheless, Simeon held his ground Sunday after Sunday, month after month, year after year, preaching God's truth directly from His Word. That is precisely what he had been wired to do, and that is what he did! Because he knew he was where he was supposed to be, doing what he was supposed to be doing, Simeon hung on.

No doubt most preachers today would imagine they had heard God's voice telling them to move on, but Simeon would have none of it. He was a different breed. He knew that God had placed him where he was in order to make a dent on the Church of England. So he stood his ground—tenaciously, stubbornly, immovably.

As a decade passed, a quiet change began to take place among the students who attended Holy Trinity. Curious by nature, they listened to Simeon carefully and liked what they heard. Unlike the drier-than-dust preachers they were used to hearing, Simeon was passionate. He was powerful. He was principled. Week after week he taught his hearers nothing but the pure, unadulterated Word of God. As a result their faith began to grow.

It didn't take long before more people began to drift in. Only they didn't come alone. They came by the dozens, by the hundreds. Before he finished his 55-year tenure as vicar of Holy Trinity, he had truly impacted a country.

He personally trained more than 1100 Anglican clergymen in the basics of preaching God's Word. While very bright, reflective, and studious, he refused to let himself become just another academician. He wanted to *know* Christ and to integrate into his life the deep significance of His crucifixion and resurrection. So he stuck to the Word. Indeed, he was so committed to teaching the Word and the Word only that he never adopted any particular theological system. He knew that if he subscribed to one system and ever found a point in Scripture that disagreed with his system, he would have to compromise the text. That was unthinkable—to alter the Bible to fit man's systems! So he avoided all systems and simply preached the truths before him exactly as he saw them developed in the Word.

Simeon also influenced people far beyond the shores of England. One young protégé, a man named Henry Martyns, had already translated the Bible into Arabic, Hindi, and Persian when he died at the age of 29. He approached his calling with the same fervor as Simeon, and applied it cross-culturally.

Charles Simeon never wavered during his entire life. He remained humble, disciplined, and keenly focused on the tasks for which God had designed him. His life is a study in the principle of being wired to win. He recognized his calling, maximized his strengths, minimized his distractions, focused himself on the finish line, and won![14]

Addicted to God

I t's one thing to read about winners and winning. It's another thing to be a winner yourself, especially when you've never thought of yourself that way. How do you win? How do you reach the goal of contentment or fulfillment or satisfaction or happiness that you seek?

At the heart of winning is something that might sound strange at first. Being a winner and winning rests on one key foundation: being addicted to God. Apart from being completely caught up in a personal relationship with God through Jesus Christ, you will never find what you seek. Augustine captured this truth beautifully centuries ago when he said to God, "My heart is restless until it finds its rest in Thee."

When you review Augustine's life you see why this statement characterized his own experience so well. In his early years God was the *last* thing on Augustine's mind. He had people to see, places to go, things to do. Besides, the pleasures of immorality were more exciting than the prospect of immortality. While Augustine's mother, Monica, was devoted to

God, he never seemed to feel the need for this same kind of relationship. Indeed, the more she pushed him toward God, the more he pulled away.

But even though he seemed hardened to God on the outside, on the inside a life-and-death battle was raging. Augustine knew that something significant was missing in his life. No matter how many physical pleasures he explored, no matter what luxuries he afforded himself, he never seemed able to gain the peace and abiding contentment that he so desired. He could mask his lack of joy only so long with his various escapades. Deep within he felt hollow. Emptiness gnawed at him like a dog on a bone.

Finally, after decades of inner agitation, on a summer morning in A.D. 386 while reading from the letters of the apostle Paul, 33-year-old Augustine gave his life to God. His life and lifestyle did not change instantaneously, but he entered into a relationship with God that quickly consumed him. Within four years of his conversion he became a priest in North Africa. Four years later he became an assistant bishop there, and one year after that he assumed the role of bishop of Hippo. He held this high and respected office until his death some 34 years later.

As bishop, Augustine pressed all his great intellect and skill into God's service, writing the significant works that would form the foundation for much of Western theology and philosophy. He poured himself into describing the essence of God, portraying well the way the Lord relates to His people. Allowing nothing God had built into his life to lie fallow, Augustine put it all to work to bring glory to His name.[1]

Why was Augustine so driven to understand and serve God as He had made Himself known in Jesus Christ? Why did he give himself to God so completely? Because he was addicted to Him. He was an all-or-nothing, no-holds-barred, sold-out God-addict!

Augustine sought peace and contentment. Like all other people, he wanted to win. Surely you can identify with this desire because everyone wants to win; everyone wants to find peace and contentment that are real and lasting.

No Trust Equals No Winning

But Augustine discovered something more than the way to eternal life. You see, winning always involves *trusting God* every day of your life. There's simply no way around it. Even those who aren't looking for their happiness in the pages of the Bible or the pew of a neighborhood church end up giving some sort of "nod to God," as incomplete and uninformed as that nod might be.

In his intriguing book *Super-Joy*, psychiatrist Paul Pearsall makes no attempt to present a Christian perspective on gaining happiness. However, as he develops his theory of how to attain "super joy," he presents a direct correlation between joy and a right relationship with God. In his own unique spin on the Ten Commandments, he writes:

> The first of the commandments ["You shall have no other gods before me"] is a prescription for faith in self and faith in God as a unified process for finding joy and health. More trips to ourselves and fewer trips to the doctor, psychologist, or self-help bookstore may be the best way to learn the joy response.[2]

No, Pearsall doesn't understand that joy demands being addicted to God as He has revealed Himself in Jesus Christ. But he does see a clear-cut relationship between God and gaining that joy.

If you were to look over the "big book" of Alcoholics Anonymous, you would find that one of the 12 steps necessary for winning is to have a dependence upon a "higher power." Again, while this higher power is left undefined (the reader is left to fill in the blank), still it is a given that if one ever wants sobriety—hence happiness, success, victory—one can only find it in relationship to God.

Over the last several years, the Gallup organization has uncovered some fascinating information in this regard. Through random polling it has demonstrated a direct correlation between the depth of someone's faith in God and that person's happiness. Gallup concludes that the more fully you are plugged into your relationship with God, the happier you will be.[3]

This same organization also discovered that those who were most caught up in their relationships with the Lord found life to be the most exciting, fulfilling, and rewarding. They suffered less stress and experienced more joy.

The simple truth is that winning is a function of addiction—addiction to God. As you are truly hooked on Him, every aspect of your life is affected positively. The psalmist truly knew what he was talking about when he said, "Blessed [happy] is the man who fears the Lord, who delights greatly in his commandments" (Psalm 112:1).

But Isn't Addiction a Bad Thing?

It's important at this point to deal with one significant objection to this idea. I'll develop this line of thought further in chapter 13 but for now let me explain my use of the term *addiction*.

The customary definition of *addiction* carries a deeply negative connotation. To use the word to describe a positive or beneficial experience creates uneasiness in many of us. We stop in our tracks because the concepts of *addict* and *God* are not normally used together.

Why? Because *addiction* has become more than a descriptive term; it also implies value. It is hence a word like *murder*. If you were to accidentally *kill* a pedestrian who jumped in front of your car late at night when you were crossing a darkened bridge, it would certainly be tragic; but it wouldn't be *murder*. Unlike *kill*, *murder* presupposes malicious intent. If you *murdered* that same man, it would mean that you decided to take his life intentionally.

If *addiction* is understood in the same pejorative sense as *murder*, it becomes difficult to consider it a good thing—especially when used in reference to a relationship with God. To get a better understanding of the problem that arises when applying *addiction* to a relationship with God, consider several current definitions of the word. While these are by no means absolute, they are a representative cross section from the field of addictive behavior, research, and discussion.

> Addiction refers to a relationship with a substance or activity that is excessive or compulsive, causes problems in one or more areas of our lives, causes distress when we are not engaging in it, and often exerts a good deal of control over our lives, even when we are not engaging in the addictive behaviors. Addiction is better seen as a "disorder" with a characteristic set of symptoms rather than something that is easily or simplistically defined.[4]

> The addict substitutes a sick relationship to an event or process for a healthy relationship with others. The addict's relationship with a mood-altering "experience" becomes central to his life.[5]

> Addiction is, essentially, a spiritual breakdown, a journey away from the truth into emotional blindness and death.[6]

> When a person is excessively devoted to something or surrenders compulsively and habitually to something, that pathological devotion becomes an addiction. The presence of a psychological and physiological dependency on a substance, relationship, or behavior results in addiction.[7]

Any cursory examination of these definitions reveals the negative understanding of the word *addiction*. Emotionally charged terms like *excessive, compulsive, disorder, spiritual breakdown*, or *pathological devotion* express a negative value about the word itself. And this is precisely the problem. While these definitions are interesting and common, they stray from the original root of the word. Thus they incorrectly color a most important aspect of life.

Our word *addiction* and its related word *addict* come from the Latin *addictus*, a past participle of *addico*. Originally the word meant merely "devoted" or "surrendered." It referred to a person given over to someone or something as a slave.

Sometimes this was against his will, as when a man became a slave to compensate for his inability to pay off a debt. At other times it was a voluntary act, as when someone surrendered himself or devoted himself totally to a teacher or leader. Whether voluntary or involuntary, however, the same result ensued. A man was totally given over to another as a slave.

With this meaning in mind, consider afresh how someone who yields himself completely to God is described in the pages of the New Testament. Both Jesus and Paul use the term *servant* or *slave* repeatedly to refer to such a person.

Jesus used this word to describe His own devotion to God. Applying a statement by the prophet Isaiah to Himself, Jesus stated: "Behold, My *Servant* whom I have chosen, my Beloved in whom My soul is well pleased" (Matthew 12:18, emphasis added).

Later, while setting the direction for the lives of His disciples, He said, "Whoever desires to be great among you, let him be your *servant*. And whoever desires to be first among you, let him be your *slave*—just as the Son of Man did not come to be *served*, but to *serve*, and to give His life a ransom for many" (Matthew 20:26-28, emphasis added).

Describing Jesus, Paul said that He willingly "made Himself of no reputation, taking the form of a *servant*, and coming in the likeness of men. And being found in appearance as a man, He humbled Himself and became obedient to the point of death, even the death of the cross" (Philippians 2:7,8, emphasis added).

There is simply no question that Jesus saw Himself as a servant (read that *slave*) of God, His Father. And Paul saw himself in the same light, had the same self-understanding. That's why he introduces himself in his letter to the Romans: "Paul, a *servant* of Jesus Christ, called to be an apostle, separated to the gospel of God" (Romans 1:1).

When Jesus and Paul spoke about being a servant, they used the Greek word *doulos*. It referred to one who was "a slave of God—subject to God, owned by Him body and soul."[8]

In many ways, *slave* is a more helpful translation today than *servant*, because it's too easy to think being a servant means merely doing another job or profession. Thus, though your job is to serve your employer, you can choose to quit. As a servant or a hired hand, you maintain your individual rights. You are free to agree or disagree about how things are to be done. If you get dissatisfied, you can look for other employment.

No such luck, however, when you're a slave. As a slave, you give up any rights you ever had. You now have no individual rights. Your life is directed as the master desires. And no longer is he seen merely as an employer; now he owns you completely. Your task is simply to do that which makes him happy. The more you tend to that, the better you do your job.

Doesn't the life of a slave sound a great deal like the description of an addict? It should. They're synonymous. Serving somebody with your whole being, being totally owned by or devoted to him, is equivalent to being completely given over to someone as a slave. A servant of God is a God-addict. To surrender to and serve God completely is to be addicted to Him.

Can't I Just Be Committed to God?

Certainly, many of us would be more comfortable with a word like *committed*. It doesn't sound so final to be "committed" to God; but somehow, being "addicted" is taking it too far. That's certainly how John W. Styll felt when he reviewed gospel singer Carmen's album *Addicted to Jesus*.

> It must be said that the title of the album is troublesome. While no one who loves Christ would dispute the notion that our love and devotion to him should be total, the concept of addiction carries extremely negative connotations. Addiction is a dysfunctional behavior, even if it's to Jesus. Furthermore, the implication that one could become "addicted" to Jesus, much like one could become addicted to drugs or alcohol, is offensive—at least to me. A relationship with Christ is not just another way to get high.[9]

Unfortunately, Styll has gotten his feet caught in the same quicksand that sucks in so many today. A go-for-broke, completely-given-over relationship with Christ is not comfortable or fitting in our cool culture. Hence we use words like *commitment*, which have come to mean very little.

Let's be honest: The word *committed* has become so diluted that it does not describe a state of total surrender or yieldedness. There are all sorts of people who would claim to be committed to God. Yet when you look at their lives and lifestyles, you see little that differs from those who claim no relationship with God. Their commitment doesn't impact their values, their spending, their use of time, or much of anything else. It is much more an intellectual decision than a total surrender of what they have and are.

No doubt you have known people who have been "committed" to several marriages, relationships that included vows obligating them to stay together "for better for worse, for richer for poorer, in sickness and in health." But the grass looked greener, or the woman looked more tantalizing, or the relationship seemed too restrictive, so that "commitment" went right out the window. Our culture instructs us to look out for ourselves. Surely you don't think that "the two shall become one flesh"?

There are even Christian attorneys today who do prenuptial agreements detailing what will happen to the property of the parties in the marriage in the case of dissolution. That's really giving up rights, isn't it? While it may once have been a helpful and meaningful term, *commitment* no longer describes the relationship with God a person needs if he is ever going to win.

The point is not where someone will spend eternity. That is a wholly separate consideration. Regardless of where someone will be eternally, the question is, "How we can experience the fulfillment, satisfaction, and wholeness we so desire *right now*?" And simple commitment won't cut it. To win demands being totally yielded to God, completely surrendered to Him; in short, addiction. You must long to serve the Lord with your whole heart. You've got to be a God-addict!

New Testament Addicts

You cannot read the New Testament and understand it apart from the centrality of servanthood. Jesus' entire life was lived in service to the Father. How else could He say something like, "I do nothing on my own but speak just what the Father has taught me. The one who sent me is with me; he has not left me alone, for I always do what pleases him" (John 8:28,29 NIV)? Why else did He willingly go to the cross, especially when He had other alternatives, attractive options, presented to Him in their most tempting forms? Why was He able to carry out His mission without giving up? Because He was consumed by living for His Father.

As he followed Jesus, Paul too was caught up in that relationship as a slave. "For to me, to live is Christ and to die is gain," he noted in his letter to the church at Philippi (Philippians 1:21 NIV). He continually subjected any self-interest to whatever would best serve the Lord. Paul was a servant, a slave, addicted to God as He revealed Himself in Jesus Christ.

And nowhere do you get the impression that for Jesus, Paul, or any of the disciples this addiction was pathological, that it somehow detracted from their health, their value as persons, or destroyed their personalities. Quite the contrary! The more fully devoted to God they were, the more healthy, complete, and whole they became. Happy were those addicted to God, for they found the fulfillment they all sought!

So will you, if you choose this "more excellent way." I know not everyone will so choose. But as you willingly allow yourself to be caught up in your relationship with Christ—as you become addicted to Him—then and only then will you be on the track toward winning. And as you press on, there is simply no doubt: You will win!

Paul:
A Case History
of a God-Addict

If ever there were a prototype of a God-addict, it would be the apostle Paul. From the moment he gave his life to Christ on the road to Damascus until he drew his last breath in Rome, he threw his life into following the Lord. Over time he learned to put everything to work for the Lord that had been built into his life by God. In other words, if ever a person was wired to win and won, it was Paul.

Paul's complete devotion to God was especially evident during his mission trip to Macedonia. To a nonbeliever his behavior would have looked nonsensical, but it simply indicated the depth of his surrender. This guy was truly addicted! If we could spend a relaxed evening with him, viewing his slides and snapshots, it would provide a perfect portrayal of his enslavement to Christ.

It wasn't even Paul's idea to go to Macedonia. He longed to visit Asia and preach the gospel there, having heard the need to bring the word of new life in Christ was very great. He wanted to be able to meet that need, so he set his course to go to Asia.

But God had other plans for Paul. As he was on his way to Asia, Paul and his companions were "forbidden by the Holy Spirit to preach the word in Asia" (Acts 16:6). It's not that God didn't want the Word preached there; rather, it's that God had that territory marked out for someone else.

After being prohibited from going into Asia, Paul picked a different spot. Again God stopped him. Exactly what method He used to block Paul's progress we do not know. We only know that it was effective and that Paul did not go. But don't assume that Paul sat around and waited for God to send him someplace! He very confidently and clearly charted his course and carried out his plan unless something got in the way. He was truly a man with a mission and assumed that, if God wanted to redirect him, He would step in when necessary.

As Paul was plotting his course, God spoke to him by means of a vision. Paul was open to listening to the Lord however He chose to manifest Himself, and this was not a singular occurrence. In the vision a man from Macedonia pleaded with Paul to come to Macedonia and bring the good news of Jesus Christ. The Macedonians were in trouble and needed help. While Paul clearly wanted to go to Asia, he was not about to miss an invitation by the Lord Himself to be involved where his services were needed so desperately. He didn't even wait for a price war on airfares; without passing "Go," he went directly to Macedonia.

The first city in which he spent time was Philippi, the foremost city in that part of Macedonia. It was a Roman colony and a military center. Unlike the other cities in the area, there were not enough Jews there to form a synagogue for Paul to use as his base.

But that didn't stop him. The moment he arrived, Paul began to teach anyway. He sought out those who gathered for prayer and instructed them about faith in Christ. On the earliest of these occasions he led a woman named Lydia into a relationship with Christ, baptized her, and was welcomed into her home. Her house then served as headquarters for the ministry in Philippi.

As Paul went about his day-to-day activities, teaching and ministering among the people, he repeatedly encountered a young slave girl who had a spirit of divination. Her "handlers" profited from her fortune-telling. As she followed Paul and his friends about, she continually cried out, "These men are the servants of the Most High God, who proclaim to us the way of salvation" (Acts 16:17). What she said was true, but it bothered Paul. He was bothered that attention was being brought to him, and he was bothered that this young girl was possessed by an evil spirit. That people would traffic in her spiritual difficulties finally agitated him to the breaking point, so one day he spun on his heels and commanded the evil spirit to come out of her in the name of Jesus Christ. And it did!

What should have been a wonderful event quickly turned ugly. Realizing they had just lost their meal ticket, the slave girl's handlers took hold of Paul and his friend Silas and dragged them to the city authorities. They charged that these Jews were trying to overturn their Roman customs and beliefs. No doubt being suspicious of "foreigners," especially Jews, the authorities had them stripped, beaten, and thrown in jail with their feet locked in stocks—all because Paul had set a woman free from a demon.

What happened next shows clearly how Paul was wired to win and was winning. His addiction was clearly exposed. In a situation that would have shut down the enthusiasm of most men, Paul took it all in stride. In fact, he didn't even seem to be discouraged. Instead, with his body raw from a whipping and his legs sore from being shackled, his voice began to echo throughout the prison with hymns of praise to God! That's right—he sang hymns while locked in stocks!

Was he crazy? No, he was completely consumed by his devotion to God and to the calling God had placed on his life. He assumed that if God had led him there, God must have something great in store for him. Why get stressed out? Why not just praise the Lord for whatever happened? In fact, why not evangelize the jailer? Imprisonment wasn't a limitation for Paul; it was another opportunity to spread the gospel, to do what he was wired to do.

We don't know if Paul and Silas hit any sour notes, but while they were singing, an earthquake occurred. It was so strong that Paul's shackles were broken and the doors of the prison opened wide. What an awesome God! What a chance to get out of this mess! But amazingly enough, Paul didn't do that. Instead, realizing that the jailer's head would be on the block if his prisoners escaped, Paul waited for him. As the jailer was about to take his own life out of fear for the punishment he expected, Paul called out to him and told him everything was okay. The prisoners hadn't moved. Everyone was present and accounted for.

Naturally, the jailer was overwhelmed by Paul's action—so much so that he and his family believed in Jesus Christ and were baptized.

Now, you tell me: How focused, how consumed, how sold-out would you have to be to feel comfortable in jail, to be so confident in the knowledge that the God who allowed you to get there in the first place would see to it that you got out? How caught up in the Lord would Paul have to have been to view his jail sentence as a blessing rather than a curse? I know many folks today who would have been rebuking the enemy for getting them into such a fix, but Paul spent his energy doing God's work. Truly, he was addicted to God!

Paul realized that he could stay in Philippi no longer, so he moved on to Thessalonica. He was there only for a short period of time—some think only a few weeks. But by the time he left, he had established a strong and vital church ready to live fully for Jesus Christ. The people had seen Paul in action. They knew what real faith looked like. None of this watered-down, Sunday-only, when-it-doesn't-get-in-the-way-of-anything-else stuff for them. They saw the real McCoy, and they determined to pattern their lives after him.

With his body still smarting from his beating in Philippi, you might think Paul would change his ways, creep into town under cover of night, and in secret meet a few interested and prequalified folks. Not so! Instead he went boldly into the local synagogue and presented the claims of Jesus Christ. Three weeks in a row he returned and made his case, putting everything into a context they would understand. Things were going fine until some of his listeners began to respond. More than a few gave their lives to Jesus Christ, and as a result, some of the disbelieving Jews got upset.

As if on cue they sought to have Paul arrested again, gathering a mob of people to attack him. This time, however, Paul was ahead of the game. Apparently at the request of his brethren, he made himself scarce. He didn't leave town, but he did hide out. When the mob finally gave up, he quietly left town at night. Yet look at what had already taken place! He had established a growing church that would prove to be a strong missionary church. Paul was doing exactly what he was designed to do and was loving it! He was home!

Leaving Thessalonica, he went directly to Berea. Once there, it was "third verse same as the first." Hardly had the dust settled from his sandals hitting town when the same folks who had stirred up trouble in Thessalonica showed up and did it all over again. Paul had already done some teaching and knew that the people were grounded in their faith in God. They diligently checked out everything he said against God's Word. Luke would come to use them as an example to other people of what it meant to live lives based on God's Word. But be that as it may, it simply was not feasible for Paul to remain among them. So he left town and proceeded to Athens.

This time he was alone. He left his cohorts in Macedonia to do the work he was unable to accomplish due to his notoriety. By his own admission when he got to Athens, he was lonely. It would have been a perfect time for him to take a little rest and relaxation and kick back. After all, nobody knew him. It would have been easy to remain anonymous in such a big city. Even though some people had heard of him, they wouldn't have recognized him. It was just what the doctor ordered—for somebody else!

Paul wasn't wired that way. He couldn't stand to sit down and shut up. He was wired to tell people about new life in Christ, and tell them he would. So he marched right into the thick of the philosophers on the Areopagus and proceeded to present the claims of Christ.

Paul's life experience had prepared him for that very moment. Educated in Jerusalem at the feet of the most noted rabbi of his day, he could hold his own in any philosophical or theological debate. He was ready for whatever might be thrown at him. No other disciple was as uniquely suited to spread the gospel in that place at that time. Peter may have been knocked off balance. James may not have fit in. But Paul was right where he was supposed to be, doing what God had wired him to do. And even though a number of those who heard him in Athens mocked, he did reach some people.

He didn't stay there long and soon moved on to Corinth where immediately he was in the thick of things. He was able to deal with some inner-church squabbles as well as preach the word of new life to those who would hear.

Remember, this was just one season in Paul's life. Yet it illustrates how he lived. He was a man who knew how God had wired him and who desired to put it to work to win. Most any evaluation of him would have to conclude he was eminently successful.

When you look at the emphasis in Paul's ministry, you see a blueprint of the way God built him. Paul emphasized balance in Christian living, doing all things decently and in order. He himself experienced almost every spiritual gifting that existed, and he understood that those gifts must always and only bring glory to God, and never to self.

He emphasized God's Word as the final authority for faith in Christ. That's why he was so fond of the Bereans. They loved God's Word, too. Never one to be caught up in the fads of the moment, no matter how "spiritual" those fads appeared, Paul brought everything back to the Word for evaluation. He never made decisions based merely on his feelings.

He emphasized the power of God as his source of strength. Pointing out that he could do nothing on his own, he reveled in the fact that he could do "all things through Christ who strengthens me" (Philippians 4:13). Whereas prior to his conversion he relied solely on his own strength, afterward he came to rely only on Christ's strength.

Paul emphasized trust in the Lord, no matter what. His very life was a testimony to that trust. No matter what his situation, he trusted God. Whether he had a lot or a little, it made no difference. As long as God was on his side, nothing else mattered. He could rest in Him!

He emphasized that God had his future in His care. That's why he could state forcefully, "For to me, to live is Christ, and to die is gain" (Philippians 1:21). He believed, taught, and practiced that God had a place with Him forever, reserved just for Paul. He reasserted continually that Jesus was coming back for all those who believed in Him, so even if his body were no longer alive, his spirit would be alive with the Lord forever!

Are you getting a picture of God-addiction?

Paul emphasized freedom. Others were quick to tie up people in the rules of religion. Paul instead stressed the relationship beneath the rules. Paul didn't do what he did because he had to; he did it because he wanted to. He believed he was free in Christ to live any way that truly brought glory to God, and suggested to others that they do likewise.

Finally, Paul emphasized winning. He believed that God had a unique place for every man and woman, that He had carefully fashioned and called each one for a special work. Nobody was left out. Nobody was unimportant. God had built people in a peculiar way to do a work that is powerful for Him. And when they were willing to throw themselves into that work unreservedly, they would find the fulfillment they sought.

That is why near the end of his life Paul could say about himself so accurately,

> I have fought the good fight, I have finished the race, I have kept the faith. Finally, there is laid up for me the crown of righteousness, which the Lord, the righteous Judge, will give to me on that Day, and not to me only but also to all who have loved His appearing (2 Timothy 4:7,8).

That is also why he could exhort those who followed Christ to run their race to win, to never settle for anything less than God's best (1 Corinthians 9:24,25).

Paul was a God-addict. As such, he had an incalculable

impact on his world and the church throughout history. Because he was truly and totally sold-out to God, he left huge footprints. He retained nothing for himself and gave all he had for God's glory. Now you tell me: Was he faithful? Was he happy? Was he fulfilled? Did he win?

Do you understand what it means to be totally yielded to God? Stay tuned. I'd like to introduce you to a couple of people you may never have met. Like Paul, they are wired to win and are winning. Perhaps God will speak to you through their lives.

The Missionaries

B ill and Penny Collier are wired to win and they are winning. Bill may have the beginning of Alzheimer's disease and may forget things more often than he would like, but when he speaks about what God has done in his life, he is as excited as ever.

Penny? She hasn't slowed down a bit. If anything, she may have speeded up. Not bad for a woman in her late sixties. I'm sure her doctor is a bit uneasy about the extra pounds she's packing around, but he would wince even more if he knew about the schedule she keeps. He would insist that it was entirely too much for one beyond "retirement age." But Penny wouldn't change a thing. You see, she knows she is exactly where God wants her to be. She knows He has carefully crafted her for her calling in life. And if she has anything to say about it, she isn't going to miss one moment of ministry. Count on it!

When you trace the strands of the intricate tapestry God has woven in the lives of both Bill and Penny, you get a better understanding of what makes them tick.

Penny Wilson became a Christian at the ripe old age of 13,

and her life was immediately and undeniably influenced by four factors: the person who led her to the Lord, the pastor who taught her, the church family who embraced her, and the Lord Himself who called her to mission work.

First, the man who led her to the Lord was an evangelist and a gospel magician. (File that fact for later reference!) The pastor under whose ministry she made the decision to follow Christ was a graduate of Wheaton College. A wonderful and loving family in the church took her in as one of their own. That's not to say she moved in with them; she didn't. But she might as well have because of the way they loved, accepted, taught, and encouraged her every step of the way in her infancy in faith. She never forgot how much that meant to her.

And then there was her call to missions. By the time she left for Wheaton College, Penny had only one thing on her mind: the mission field. She felt that God was calling her to be a missionary. Further, if things worked out she planned to carry out this calling in the jungles of the Belgian Congo (modern-day Zaire).

Through college she fueled her vision with missionaries and their stories. Whenever the opportunity presented itself to rub shoulders with these modern-day apostles, she was there. She desired to taste whatever morsels they had to offer. Interestingly enough, one of the fellows she dated in college was a young man who was also sold-out and mission-minded. His name was Jim Elliott. In a few years he would become one of the most famous missionaries in modern history as he laid down his life for the Lord on a river bank in Ecuador, attempting to take the gospel to the Auca Indians (for a further description, see the book *Through Gates of Splendor*).

After her conversion, Penny never knew a stranger. The once-shy little girl was transformed overnight. It was as though she had stuck her finger in a light socket and God turned on the juice. Her outgoing and gregarious personality, coupled with her zeal to share Christ, made a very effective evangelist. Every opportunity she had, with every talent and skill and even fractional ability she possessed, she would reach out in Jesus' name. She learned how to use puppets to bring

God's message to children, and even taught herself how to play the marimba so she could accompany any singing. In her spare time she led one of the early Young Life groups as well. Why not? Who needed sleep? She could do that any old time!

The summer after she graduated from college, Penny was asked to lead a vacation Bible school for a church in Florida. So, packing up her trusty marimba and puppets, she made the trek from Illinois down south to minister God's love to a bunch of kids she had never seen. Though it was still in the United States, it was like a missions trip, far beyond anything she had known.

Her time in Florida went extremely well—so well that representatives from a mission in Cuba who happened to catch one of her presentations asked if she would come and minister there. What a question! Didn't she have "reserved for missions" written all over her? Of course she would love to come and minister. There was only one problem. Leading vacation Bible school didn't generate much income, so she had no money and no prospect of earning enough for such a trip.

When the church in Florida heard about her opportunity, they leaped at the chance to help. They told her they would finance her trip. She didn't need to spend precious time fundraising. All she needed to do was pack her things and be off to Cuba. It took about two heartbeats and a packed marimba and Penny was off and running.

By the time Penny returned to the United States, she was hooked on missions. There was no question in her mind: She would be a missionary. With perfect peace in her heart and certainty in her mind, she approached her denominational headquarters and asked them about the next steps toward fulfilling her dream. "You need to go to seminary," they replied without looking up from the desk.

More years and more classes might have stopped others, but not Penny. She knew God had placed this desire in her heart and had given her the tools to be effective wherever she might go. So seminary it was. She pursued a master's degree in Christian Education from Northern Baptist Seminary in Chicago.

While working on her graduate degree she met a fellow student named Bill Collier who was enrolled in the undergraduate program. Although they were the same age, he was behind her academically due to several years in the Armed Forces during World War II. It was pretty amazing that he had made it this far, given that he had to drop out of high school as a junior. But after earning his G.E.D. (general equivalency diploma), he was allowed to enter the undergraduate program to study for the ministry.

Over the next several years Bill and Penny entered into an on-again, off-again relationship. They both were deeply devoted to the Lord and desired to give themselves unreservedly to Him. They also shared the same vision for ministry. But there was something about their relationship that needed seasoning. So, while Bill continued his education, Penny went off with a new graduate degree to get some practical experience in a local church as director of Christian Education. In those days, that position really meant "the one who does whatever the pastor either can't or doesn't want to," so Penny got a firsthand feel for serving the Lord in the trenches. She yearned to be closer to Bill, but they both had so many tasks to attend to that it just never seemed to come together.

For a while the couple didn't even correspond. When Penny assumed that their relationship was over, out of nowhere she received a letter from Bill. One thing led to another (or in this case two things led to each other) and in no time they were married. Now they were free to pursue their dreams as husband and wife, a couple completely consumed with serving Christ on the mission field. They would be lethal for the Lord! They were so sure that this was where God wanted them that they had themselves dedicated for this purpose at their wedding. No equivocation here!

Now it was Bill's turn to go to seminary. The denomination hadn't changed its mind about the need for graduate education for its missionaries. Thus, Bill and Penny headed west for Portland, Oregon, and another seminary program.

While Bill went to school, Penny worked at World Vision in the adoption department. Under her direction, World Vision developed its sponsorship program which would come to be one of its best-known ministries. As a result of the contacts she made and the needs Bill and Penny felt as a couple, they ended up adopting two Korean orphans. In fact, they were the first Americans allowed to adopt foreign children by proxy, which was only made possible by a special act of the United States Congress.

They were no longer the dynamic duo. Now they were a full-fledged family of four! You would think that juggling all of those responsibilities would have kept them busy. But not Bill and Penny. Not only did they keep all those balls in the air, but they added another one as well. On weekends they decided to help out a little church about a hundred miles away from Portland. It was too small to afford a pastor and could only give Bill five dollars a week, which hardly paid for his gas. But in a way, this was a mission. And that's what their lives were about, what they had been dedicated for. Even though the whole family had to sleep in the car every weekend, that was of little concern. They were serving the Lord, and they were happy. How can you beat that?

By the time he finished school, Bill had both a master's degree and a teaching credential. He had a feeling that the latter might come in handy. You never know what you might need out there on the mission field, or how long it would be once they got to the Congo before they returned for their first furlough.

Unfortunately, the problem never developed. Bill and Penny never reached the Congo. As he was nearing the end of his educational experience, Bill flunked a physical examination required by his denomination for all potential missionary candidates. He wasn't actually unhealthy; he just had some potential problems that could flare up at any time. Though the denomination liked him a lot, it concluded Bill was too much of a risk to invest the time and money and effort to put him out in the field only to have to bring him home.

Put yourself in Bill and Penny's shoes. If you had just completed years of training and praying and planning for the time you would be serving the Lord as a missionary, how would you feel if your file were suddenly labeled "mission impossible"? Would you call it quits? Would you be angry with God? Would you give up your faith?

Praying about the next step, the young couple came to a clear consensus. It was the mission field they had trained for, and to the mission field they would go! It just wouldn't be the foreign mission field. Instead, they would go to rural communities and small churches that couldn't afford pastors. They could support themselves by teaching school so the churches wouldn't need to worry about meeting a salary they were unable to pay.

With that in mind they moved to the little town of Dee, Oregon, where Bill already had been pastoring. When they arrived, he got a job teaching school at Petersberg School, a small country school that had lots of Celilo Indian students. In a way it was like being on the mission field he had dreamed of. There were certainly times he was having a "cross-cultural experience"! On the side he pastored the church, complete with preaching, calling, counseling, marrying, and burying. While he was invested in all of this, Penny went back to school so she could add a teaching credential to her other educational accomplishments and degrees. That way she could join Bill in the teaching enterprise.

As time went on and as their little church grew, they were asked to come and help out another church, this time in Ione, Oregon. It was the oldest Baptist church in the state, but it had been closed due to lack of attendance and support. The problem this church faced wasn't that it was too small; it was nonexistent! Some people in the community were mature Christians and believed this church could get a new start if only somebody would pastor it. Since Bill and Penny had built up the church at Dee to the point it could support a full-time pastor, they felt free to make a change. While others might have rejoiced that they could now quit teaching and "minister full-time," that was not Bill and Penny. After all, this was their mission field. They decided to accept this new challenge, assuming the position as a call from the Lord.

With the change of churches came a change in residence. They moved to Arlington, where they both got teaching jobs.

Bill taught the first grade, Penny the fourth. Again, on the side, they jump-started the little church that had been a museum.

While serving the church in Ione, Bill got an opportunity to do an evangelistic crusade in Korea. Given his long-standing interest in missions and his two Korean children, his heart leaped at the opportunity. His pocketbook, however, told him it wasn't an option. Some of the local wheat farmers became aware of his plight, however, and came up with the money necessary to get him there and back. Even before he had a chance to figure out how it was all going to come together, he was headed across the Pacific to Korea.

While there, Bill accomplished much more than a success-ful preaching mission. He also arranged to take five children back to the States with him for adoption. Two for one family, two for another, and one for himself! Meanwhile, back at the ranch, Penny knew nothing of what was transpiring. Evidently she was listening to the Lord, however, because on the way to the airport to welcome Bill home, she stopped by the store and picked up some diapers. Good thing. They were pressed into service immediately!

While ministering in Korea, Bill met a Norwegian mis-sionary who was as sold-out to Christ as he was. But this brother in Christ had a problem. His children needed to con-tinue their secondary education and it wasn't possible where they were. Was there any way Bill could help him out? Assur-ing the poor fellow that God must have a way, Bill returned home.

God had a way, all right. Bill worked the wheat fields in the summer and saved all the money he earned so that he could pay for the tickets to bring the Norwegian twins over to live with his family. That way they could continue their education. Again, this would incur no small cost. By the time the Nor-wegian twins rejoined their parents, they had lived with Bill and Penny three and one-half years. But it wasn't a burden; it was a blessing.

I think it's time to review Bill and Penny's situation: five children, teaching school, pastoring a church. (Oh, I forgot to mention that Bill's mother also had moved in.) A full plate, wouldn't you say? Not for the Colliers. In addition to all this, they decided to accept a new call to pastor another needy church at Trout Lake, which was 100 miles away.

They kept their teaching and living situations as they were and commuted on the weekends, just like old times. Only now there were eight of them packed into the car. But then, who's counting? Sundays were a joy for the Collier family—even when considering that the Sunday evening service didn't end until 10:00 P.M. and the eight Colliers still had a 100-mile drive ahead of them. The hard part was getting up Monday morning to teach school.

Were they complaining? Hah! This is exactly what God had wired them to do, and they were doing it with all their hearts. Each and every step of the way, God blessed. Don't get me wrong. It wasn't easy. They went without things that others call "necessities." Yet none of that mattered to them because they were "home." They were in the center of God's will for their lives, doing what He had designed them to do. They were winning.

After a year or so of "sardine sojourning," the Colliers moved their whole family to Trout Lake. They wanted to be part of the community in which their church was located. Hence Bill got a teaching job in town and Penny got one about 15 miles away. It took 15 years to build the church to a size that could support a full-time pastor. During those years God used Bill and Penny to do a unique kind of mission work in a community that had more cows than people. God was using them just like they thought He wanted to. As long as they were willing to stick to His plan, things just seemed to work.

When he felt he was nearing the end of his time at Trout Lake, Bill was asked to consider a little church in Stevenson. Did I say "little"? Can you call a church with nine women and one man "little"? "Microscopic" is more like it. Whatever you might call it, this church was hurting. To get a feel for the situation, Bill preached there one Sunday morning, visited the people that afternoon, and knew by evening that God was calling him to be with these people. They would never have a preacher if he and Penny didn't come. It was that simple. So they went.

Again he got a teaching job in nearby Skamania. This time, however, he also served as principal. Imagine—he got his credential so he would be ready for whatever God might call him to do, and now he was a teaching principal! Once again, while God put bread on their table by their teaching, they nursed that little church to health. It also became strong enough to support a full-time pastor by the time they left.

Finally, Bill's health caught up with him and forced him to step down from his pastorate. He moved to Vancouver and taught there until his retirement, continuing to be extremely active in a church, teaching Sunday school, and ministering wherever he could.

At the same time Penny began to come into her own in ministry. It was as if she had been passed a baton. To be sure, she had been running the race all along right beside Bill. She was no less involved and using everything God had given her all the way. She was taking new Christians under her wing at the same time she was reaching out to other people who did not know the Lord. She was about God's work the entire time. But now it became obvious that she was being asked to turn the heat up a notch.

As Penny hearkened back to the early days in her faith and remembered how profoundly she was influenced by the evangelist who preached and used gospel magic, she felt led to develop the same type of ministry. She recognized that it had accomplished great things in her own life and sensed it could be powerful in the lives of other people.

Being accustomed to small towns and smaller churches, she had a clear sense of what needed to be done. She was comfortable going into any kind of area and her demands were few. So after establishing a linkage with the Salvation Army, she suddenly found herself on a circuit, presenting puppet shows, gospel magic, and evangelistic crusades for kids in Salvation Army outposts up and down the West Coast. When asked to minister the good news of Jesus Christ to those who didn't know Him, like Paul, she said, "When do I start?"

With a husband like Bill and the ministry that they had shared across the years, Penny was ready for just about anything. When she was asked to go to Alaska and minister, she drove that long, lonely highway in a van with more than 150,000 hard miles on it. With her equipment, rabbits, doves, and marimba to keep her company, she went wherever she was called, thrilled that God had a special place reserved just for her.

Even now things haven't changed much for the Colliers. Penny continues to serve the Lord every chance she gets. No, it's not her vocation; it's her life! It's Bill's, too. He may not be able to be as active today as he was even five years ago, but he has run the race flat out.

Could Bill and Penny have had an easier life? Sure! Would Bill have had fewer health problems if they had chosen a more placid path? Maybe. But would they have won? No way!

Bill and Penny knew what they were wired to do. Originally, they thought it would be in Africa where they would give themselves totally for the Lord. But it turned out God had need for them much closer to home. As long as they were faithful to yield themselves totally to God, being available for whatever He wanted to do, God would use them to do a mighty work.

The Colliers understand what it means to be wired to win. They also know what winning feels like. All it takes is total surrender to God!

A Life That Works Right

Addicted to God. Does the very concept frighten you? Does it sound like too much of a good thing? As far as John Prince, Patty Stephens, and Bill and Penny Collier are concerned, a person could never get too much of God. In fact, the more caught up they became in their relationships with the Lord, the more exciting, fulfilling, and challenging their lives came to be.

Guess what? When you are addicted to God, the same thing will happen to you. Why? Because that's how God designed you to work.

Although this may surprise you, you *are* addicted to something or someone right now. Whatever you are addicted to is either building you up or tearing you down—right now.

What the Bible has to say about this is downright frightening. First, Jesus says, "Most assuredly, I say to you, whoever commits sin is a slave of sin" (John 8:34). *So far so good*, you might think. After all, you're no axe-murderer. You haven't embezzled millions or sprayed a playground with bullets. So far you're safe. Or are you? Paul writes, "For all have sinned and fall short of the glory of God" (Romans 3:23).

Wait a minute! Wouldn't that include you? Isn't Paul saying that there is not a person alive who is free from sin, who has lived a perfect life? Yes, that's exactly what he's saying. And when you think about it, don't you have to agree?

The Delete Key and You

My computer has a button labeled "delete." No matter what I type on my screen, if I merely highlight a section and press this button, whatever is highlighted vanishes like magic! It's fantastic—unless I hit the delete key by mistake.

Wouldn't it be wonderful to have such a button for your life? If you made a mistake, if you spoke before thinking or acted before considering the consequences, you could just hit your "delete" button and all the negative fallout would disappear. Wouldn't that be great?

The only reason you are nodding your head is because you can recall all sorts of instances in which you would have hit that button. That means that you agree with Paul: You are a sinner. Like everyone else you know, you've done things that fall into the less-than-God's-best category. Everyone has a bent toward sinning. Since the time of Adam and Eve, it's been a part of our nature.

If you disagree with this, take a glance around you. Read this morning's newspaper. Listen to the news on your radio or television. The philosophy that "every day, in every way, man is getting better and better" is not proving true. Instead, mankind continues in its sinful ways, second verse worse than the first.

With all the revelations of child abuse and the subsequent reports of punishment inflicted on the perpetrators, wouldn't you think such abuse would come to a screeching halt? Yet just last week in my own community another father was found guilty of killing his own child by means of physical abuse. How is that possible in 1992?

Even heads of state don't seem to learn from experience. Didn't it strike you as strange that after having been almost wiped out through Operation Desert Storm, Iraq just a few months later was acting as if the war had never happened? There Iraq was, barring United Nations personnel from viewing certain facilities within Baghdad and denying reports of rearming while at the same time receiving military shipments from North Korea. What does it take? Obliterating the city of Baghdad? Paving all of Iraq?

If mankind is truly getting better, is free from sin, why do we read such things as the following, which appeared in a local newspaper?

> In May, the Capital Security Command in Bangkok, Thailand, established a "coup d'etat" hotline. People wanting to check out rumors can call 240-2111 to see whether there has been a revolution.[1]

Yes, what Paul says is clearly true: "All have sinned and fall short of the glory of God." What began in the Garden as an innocent little taste test is still going strong today.

A Bad Way to Lose Your Life

As we continue in our sin, refusing to admit or confess it, let alone forsake it, our very life is stolen from us. As David said in Psalm 32:3,4 about the effect of sin in his own life, "When I kept silent, my bones grew old through my groaning all the day long. For day and night Your hand was heavy upon me; my vitality was turned into the drought of summer."

Paul takes the consequence of living in sin one step further. "The wages of sin is death," he states (Romans 6:23). If you sin, you die. There is no way around it. And if what Jesus says is true—that when we commit sin we're enslaved to it—then all of us are in big trouble! Not a very cheery thought. Especially when it ends in death.

Sin promises one thing and produces another. Drugs promise to expand your mind and end up shrinking it. Booze promises relaxation and instead increases anxiety. Illicit sex promises pleasure and produces pain, shame, remorse, and disease. Oddly enough, built right into sin itself is the feeling that if you do it "just once more," then you will be satisfied. Then you'll be happy. Then you will experience relief. But once you repeat your sin of choice, instead of feeling better, you feel worse.

Recently a television documentary dealt with the plight of individuals addicted to gambling. One sad story stood out. It featured a man who could have been your next-door neighbor. He could have been you. He didn't live far from Atlantic City, where gambling is legal, so it was easy for him to get casually drawn in.

It was no big deal when he began gambling. Oh, he lost a few bucks, but nothing big—nothing that would take a divot out of his lifestyle. Nothing that would cause him grief or attract the attention of his wife. He just did it for fun, as a way to relax, kind of like playing golf.

But this particular hobby soon began to control him. He thought about it day and night. Just thinking about it would give him a "rush," start the chemistry of his body changing, get him excited. Once that occurred, his only hope to resolve the growing tension was to go to the tables and put a few bucks on the line. Besides, this time he would probably win. Think what he could do when he hit it big. Imagine what people would think of him when he was really in the chips!

As the days, weeks, and months rolled by, his habit grew. Before he knew it, his gambling was hopelessly out of control. The stakes were always bigger. Though he never admitted it, he was enslaved to gambling. Think about that—*a slave!*

The stakes continued to get higher until he finally lost almost everything. He had tapped out all of his accounts and run all of his credit cards to the limit. The only thing left to bet was his house. Since he knew his wife wasn't aware of his activities, he had to forge her signature to the title. Then he could put it on the line for that big win. Surely this time he could recoup all his other losses.

Only it didn't happen. As usual, he lost. The numbers told him the awful truth, and he broke out in a cold sweat. He began to shake. He wanted to vomit. Why did this have to happen? What could he possibly do now? How could he get out of this?

He needed time to think. He just knew there had to be a way. But as he quickly plotted his next move, events took a nasty turn. Not knowing that her husband had lost title to their home, his wife had decided it was time for them to "move up," to sell their house and buy a new one. Little did she know that they had nothing to sell!

Backed against a wall, this gambling slave devised a scheme and carried it out. He kidnapped the young son of a neighbor and held him for $500,000 ransom. Imagine that— so caught up in his addiction that he thought he could get away with something that outrageous, that stupid. But when you're enslaved to sin, it blinds you and lures you toward your own destruction. You dig your own grave and don't even know you're holding the shovel. You get caught in a downward spiral right into the pits of hell itself.

Of course the kidnapping didn't work. The gambler was caught and imprisoned . . . locked up . . . jailed with murderers, rapists, child molesters, and embezzlers—but only for six months. This was his first offense, after all.

When the television reporter visited him in prison, she asked what he had learned while locked up and how he was progressing in his "recovery" program. "Oh," he replied, "they haven't put me into any programs. I'm just doing my time." The surprised reporter then asked what he thought he would do when he got out. Would he stay as far away as possible from the activity that had put him behind bars?

His answer rocked her back on her heels: "Actually, probably the first thing I'll do when I get out is to get back to those tables! Don't you understand? When you put your money down on that table, you're really somebody!"

Unbelievable. He hadn't learned a thing. No doubt he would go from bad to worse and all because he had bought into the lie: Feed the habit and you will be happy. You'll be a winner!

Do you see how an addiction to anything other than God will tear you down?

Same Story, Different Cast

The stories of those who have become enslaved to drugs

feature great similarities. Drug addiction usually starts out "recreationally," with no plan to get hooked. A familiar comment about the use of drugs is, "Oh, I just do this for fun. I can quit anytime! I'm not hooked on this or anything!" Yet where does it always lead?

I once counseled a young man addicted to illicit sexual behavior. For him it began with voyeurism, becoming a Peeping Tom. He said it was fun to spy on some of the young women in his neighborhood at night when they didn't know he was looking. He would creep into their backyards and hope that they didn't fully shut their shades when they got ready for bed. Then he would watch while they undressed. Boy, did that ever excite him—for a while.

Then he needed to add a new dimension to enjoy the same "rush." He needed to be in a position where he might be caught: not hide in the bushes quite as deeply, be a little less careful going into the backyard. He needed this new twist in order to experience the same level of excitement that he used to get by peeking in the windows.

Soon even that wasn't enough. So he began to expose himself. Like his career as a Peeping Tom, he began in hidden places, places that gave him an easy escape. He would "flash and run." Finally, however, even that wasn't enough to pick him up, to release the internal chemicals he had come to depend on. So he had to do it in public places. And on and on it went as his life spiraled ever downward. What began as a "harmless little peek" on a neighbor turned into a nightmare, a daymare, a lifemare.

That's the way most addictions work. They form a cycle, a vicious cycle, a cycle that tears you down piece by piece. Ultimately every area of your life is affected.

The Robber Who Can't Be Jailed

Illicit addictions rob you of your health. Ever heard of anyone dying of cirrhosis of the liver due to the excessive use of alcohol?

Illicit addictions rob you of your mental faculties. Ever known anyone whose brain was "fried" from excessive use of drugs? Ever known anyone who could no longer concentrate due to being in an alcohol- or drug-induced stupor? While many groups tout the facility of certain drugs to expand the mind, quite the reverse is true. As one expert stated so well:

> Scientifically, these alterations of perceptual reality are the result of self-imposed changes in the delicate electrochemical balance of the brain. The schism between science and the heart is perhaps most evident when a "flower child" resists the notion that his or her cherished drug experiments are simply mucking up or crudely interfering with natural brain functions.[2]

Illicit addictions rob you of your future. Ever thought about what the people who stop you for a handout might have accomplished? Are there masterpieces that have not been painted or medical cures that have not been discovered because someone took a wrong turn?

Illicit addictions rob you of your dignity. Ever known anyone who felt good about frequenting pornographic bookstores or massage parlors? Ever known someone who was proud to list those activities as hobbies on a resumé? If you were consumed by such habits, would you reveal it in the message on your answering machine? "Sorry, I can't come to the phone right now—I'm down at 'Sleazy Eddies' renting a couple of XXX flicks for the evening"!

The Phenomenal Benefits of God-Addiction

While an addiction to anything other than God tears you down, the reverse is also true. An addiction to God will build you up! In every way you can imagine, it will enable you to win.

It all hinges on your relationship with Jesus Christ. He is God's provision to take care of your sin, once and for all. In His death on the cross He took your place, paid the price for your sin and for the sin of everyone who would believe in Him. While Paul says that all sinners deserve the death sentence, he also says, "The gift of God is eternal life in Christ Jesus our Lord" (Romans 6:23).

When you enjoy a relationship with God through Christ, you have the opportunity to rise above the sin that has threatened to sink you. That doesn't mean that you won't sin. But it does mean that you won't *have* to.

As you realize you are free from the downward pull of sin, you will become aware of a whole new life opening up for you. As you then desire to become everything you were designed to be, you will grab all that God offers you to rise above your sin. You'll rely on His power. You'll follow His Word. You'll seek His counsel. You'll live His life. In short, in this new relationship, you'll yield yourself totally to Him. You'll become a God-addict not because you have to, but because you want to.

The more you are consumed by your life in Christ, the more it will touch every facet of your being. It will have a positive effect on your mind. Indeed, the only way to be addicted to God is to allow your mind to be immersed in and shaped by His truth. "Do not be conformed to this world," Paul says in Romans 12:2, "but be transformed by the renewing of your mind, that you may prove what is that good and acceptable and perfect will of God."

While the "truths" of man change as quickly as new shipments to the bookstore, God's truths endure. "The grass withers, the flower fades, but the word of our God stands forever" (Isaiah 40:8). Thus, fixing your mind on His truths will affect the way you approach your whole life. That is the one key reason why Paul stated so emphatically:

> "Finally, brethren, whatever things are true, whatever things are noble, whatever things are just, whatever things are pure, whatever things are lovely, whatever things are of good report, if there is any virtue and if there is anything praiseworthy— meditate on these things" (Philippians 4:8).

As you fix your mind on God's unchanging truths, your physical health will benefit. You will be refreshed, renewed, regenerated. Don't misunderstand. Faithfulness to God and His truth does not guarantee good health. Trusting Christ for life isn't an automatic cure-all for cancer, high blood pressure, or tennis elbow. All other things being equal, however, keeping your mind stayed on God's truths will have a very salutary effect on your physical being.

You will suffer less stress and anxiety. Why? Because truths like those expressed by Jesus in John 14:27 will be operative in your life. "Peace I leave with you, My peace I give to you; not as the world gives do I give to you. Let not your heart be troubled, neither let it be afraid." Or while you know that you have some major difficulties facing you, you will still be confident knowing "that all things work together for good to those who love God, to those who are the called according to His purpose" (Romans 8:28).

Wonderful physical benefits also will result from having a mind immersed in and fixed on God's truth. Solomon expressed some of these benefits so well in Proverbs. "A sound heart is life to the body, but envy is rottenness to the bones" (Proverbs 14:30). "A merry heart makes a cheerful countenance, but by sorrow of the heart the spirit is broken" (Proverbs 15:13). "All the days of the afflicted are evil, but he who is of a merry heart has a continual feast" (Proverbs 15:15). In short, "a merry heart does good, like medicine, but a broken spirit dries the bones" (Proverbs 17:22).

God continually insists that you can find all that you seek by being caught up in your life with Him. Jesus made that relationship completely accessible to anyone who would desire it, and you, too, can enter in. You will enjoy the fulfillment of His promises and see for yourself that He really does love, accept, cleanse, empower, protect, teach, gift, enable, guide, provide and give eternal life to all those who love Him. With that as a rock-solid base, you have the foundation for winning, for experiencing real fulfillment and wholeness.

In the book of Nehemiah, God's people were up against seemingly impossible odds and yet found that the joy of the Lord was their strength (Nehemiah 8:10). It is that very joy that grows in your life as you are addicted to God. Hence, your strength develops day by day.

God built us to be fueled by this joy. The Bible teaches that the more joy we have, the better we work. The reverse is also true. A critical spirit, complaining, factiousness, backbiting, gossip, and negativity in general are an abomination to God because they destroy the very thing He so desires to build up. Again and again He says to avoid any and all of these destructive tendencies. Instead He points us to develop everything that contributes to a joyful heart, a peaceful and contented spirit.

Science Discovers God's Handiwork

Only recently have social scientists begun to "discover" what God created long ago. Though they rarely discern His hand in the overall design of things, they do recognize certain principles in His overall scheme. They see that living a life filled with joy enriches and enhances one's life immeasurably. They see that joy makes the brain work better. Sound strange? Well, it's true!

> Smiling and laughter are ways of voluntarily giving the brain an oxygen shower. When we smile, our facial muscles contract to increase the blood flow to our brains. Our tears of laughter at the end of a laughing spell are ways of relieving the buildup of blood supply to the brain.[3]

> When these activities stimulate your brain, it functions better. They help new neural pathways to go to work and lay a foundation for strength.[4]

In addition to making your brain work better, a joyful life makes your body function better. In his book *Head First*, author Norman Cousins states:

> Medical researchers at a dozen or more medical centers have been probing the effects of laughter on the human body and have detailed a wide array of beneficial changes—all the way from enhanced respiration to increases in the number of disease-fighting immune cells. Extensive experiments have been conducted, working with a significant number

of human beings, showing that laughter contributes to good health. Scientific evidence is accumulating to support the biblical axiom that "a merry heart doeth good like a medicine."[5]

Or, as Dr. William Fry, Jr., of Stanford Medical School, says about laughter:

> It causes huffing and puffing, accelerates the heart rate, raises blood pressure, speeds up breathing, increases oxygen consumption, gives the muscles of the face and stomach a workout, and relaxes muscles not involved in laughing. Liver, stomach, pancreas, spleen, and gall bladder are all stimulated. In short, your entire system gets an invigorating lift.[6]

Finally, a rationale for enjoying Peter Sellers and all the Pink Panthers! A joyful heart also works to the benefit of our immune system:

> Our body's immune system fights disease more effectively when we are happy rather than depressed. When we are depressed, the number of certain disease-fighting cells declines. Stressed animals and distressed people are therefore more vulnerable to various illnesses.[7]

Getting even more specific about this physiological consequence of living a life of joy, Pearsall says:

> The best immune system booster is a shot of super joy. Research in the new field of psychoneuroimmunology clearly demonstrates that our emotions are related to the functioning of our immune systems. It is a fact that how we feel affects when and how we get sick and get well. Super joy is a joy that results in immunoenhancement. Joyful people get sick less often and less seriously than unjoyful people, and when they do get sick, they more readily mobilize their own natural healing powers.[8]

If that's not enough for you, think about this. Reporting an interview with a Jewish survivor of a German concentration camp in World War II, psychiatrist Pearsall says,

> "I can still feel the way I felt in that camp," reported Clare. "There was a certain invigoration, even though it was hell. It's as though God gave me something to ease the pain." Clare is describing in this statement her own pretested psychochemicals, which protected her in this threatening situation, lifting her and energizing her even when her environment was the ultimate in stress and pain.

> The joy response is prewired into the human system. Like a new home with wiring for phones that have not been installed, the joy response circuitry is going largely unused, or at least is underused. The healing psychochemicals produced within the brain are there for us, but we must make connection with them.[9]

This just scratches the surface of the physical benefits of a joyful spirit. There are also emotional benefits. The more joyful you are, the more hopeful you are. The more hopeful, the more peaceful. The more peaceful, the better you get along with others, the better you end up feeling about yourself. Much research has shown that in contrast to people who lack joy, happy people

> are strikingly energetic, decisive, flexible, creative, and sociable. Compared to unhappy people, they are more trusting, more loving, more responsive [and] tolerate more frustration. They are less likely to be abusive and are more lenient. Whether temporarily or enduringly happy, they are more loving and forgiving and less likely to exaggerate or overinterpret slight criticism. They choose long-term rewards over immediate pleasures.[10]

Contrary to what some seem to think, we are not just a hunk of flesh and a piece of bone. As humans, we didn't just show up, with no desire for meaning, purpose, or direction. Built deep within each one of us is the desire to win—to have peace, satisfaction, fulfillment, contentment, and joy. God has wired us that way. But the only way we'll ever find it and *win* is by trusting Him, yielding to Him completely. Only as we are sold-out God-addicts will we ever become winners.

As Isaiah stated so beautifully: "Those who wait on the LORD shall renew their strength; they shall mount up with wings like eagles, they shall run and not be weary, they shall walk and not faint" (Isaiah 40:31).

The Prayer Warrior

Margaret Loos looked resplendent in her beautiful royal-blue dress. Her white hair glistened like fresh-fallen snow on a moonlit night. She was stunning!

She had prayed about this day and anticipated it for years. And now at age 70, after walking her only daughter, Joy, down the aisle, Margaret sat and watched as her little girl was joined in marriage to a handsome young man. The ceremony proceeded like clockwork. The little country church was decorated beautifully. The various personnel did exactly what they were supposed to do. The accompanist, the pastor, the wedding party, and guests were pleased to witness this joyous occasion.

Almost as quickly as it began, it was over. Well . . . almost over. Margaret watched with a mixture of gladness and sadness as the pastor pronounced the giddy young couple husband and wife. She had longed for this very moment and yet things would now be different forever. Her daughter would be moving far away to Alaska. But it was exactly what she had been praying for this very day, this very moment.

As the couple kissed, the accompanist began his lead-in for the recessional, a tune familiar to most everyone present. Almost instinctively they began to hum the words of the song:

> You shall go out with joy, and be
>   led forth with peace;
> the mountains and the hills
>   will break forth before you.
> There'll be shouts of joy,
>   and all the trees of the field
> Will clap, will clap their hands. [1]

Just as the newlyweds began to descend the little staircase to leave the sanctuary, it happened. Margaret—beautiful, radiant, dignified Margaret, with eyes twinkling and her face ready to explode from the expanse of her smile—leaped to her feet. In one motion, she raised a tambourine above her head, twirled about in place, and began to dance down the aisle in front of the bride and groom! The joy that she expressed so naturally and freely was infectious, and everyone in attendance was drawn into the celebration. The entire place spontaneously erupted into laughter and applause as Margaret led the bridal party back down the aisle.

But wait . . . it wasn't over! No sooner had she finished escorting the happy couple out than she was back. She danced right up the aisle to the front, spun around a time or two, shook her tambourine, and danced back out again.

Now that's what you call joy! That is what happiness looks like. If anybody deserved to celebrate that day, Margaret did. This moment had been a long time in coming.

Margaret's life began in turmoil. A few months before she and her twin sister were born, Margaret's mother, Elsie, left her husband in Mobile, Alabama. Though he was a pastor and she was immersed in the life of the church, she could no longer deal with his womanizing. His last relationship was the final straw. She packed up her five children and moved back to her family home on Utilla Island, Republic of Spanish Honduras, Central America.

Four months later when the twins were born, Elsie had to deal with the hardship of being 40 years old and a single parent with seven children to rear. Had she been unable to move into her parents' home, life would have been unbearable.

For the children, growing up on the island was paradise. With luscious tropical fruit always within reach and a grandpa who was a soft touch for pennies to buy pink coconut candy or fudge, what could be more ideal?

The scene changed a few years later when a new stepfather stepped into the picture. Mr. Mattie moved the family to the opposite side of the island where he owned a big house with a harbor in front and a lagoon in back, complete with alligators. That was home for a few years, until they moved to La Ceiba. Because he was involved with the Standard Fruit Company, the kids got to attend the company school, use the company health services, and, best of all, take part in the company social life. They got to accompany the various tourist excursions through the jungle and swim on the special beaches reserved for their parties. Even as youngsters they got to attend the formal dances.

But there was a definite downside to Margaret's life. Over time, Mr. Mattie began to verbally abuse her mother, especially for her faith in God. On one occasion he became so angry with his wife that he shredded her Bible with his machete. Despite all that, Elsie somehow managed to keep her faith. There was nothing and nobody that would get in the way of her faith in the Lord.

No matter how difficult life became for her, Elsie was constant in prayer and involvement in the life of her church. She didn't even attend the church fitting for someone of her stature. Instead she chose to take part in a poor, almost all-black Methodist church in the middle of the cantinas and prostitutes. Though it might embarrass the children to accompany her there, it was never an option to do otherwise.

While Margaret didn't know it at the time, God was investing in a special kind of bank account for her from which she would draw deeply throughout her life. He was depositing in her account the gifts of dogged faith in Himself and constancy in prayer that marked the life of her mother and would become the hallmarks of Margaret's life. Although Margaret would stray greatly from her relationship with the Lord, already a base was being established for the future.

Margaret and a sister eventually grew tired of what they considered a restrictive life with their mother and moved to Guatemala to live with another sister and her husband. Life was easy for them there, what with four live-in servants! Since even that got boring after a while, Margaret taught herself to type, which later qualified her for a secretarial position. In addition, while plying her trade as a secretary, she found she was able to cope with the constant hassle of a man's world.

Margaret quickly enmeshed herself in the social life of the area. While still in her teens she began enjoying cocktails and a fast pace of life. While she was hospitalized with one of her quarterly attacks of malaria, her longtime doctor said to her: "Margarita, you would die if I let you. If you do not change your style of living, you will not live through your twenties!" But like other people that age, Margaret considered herself invincible. She enjoyed her lifestyle and had no desire to change. So as soon as she was well enough, she got back into the swing of things.

A few years later she left Guatemala to rejoin her mother in New Orleans. If she thought her mom was devoted to God before, she hadn't seen anything! Now her mom was a live-wire Southern Baptist, the kind who would witness to anything that moved—animal, vegetable, or mineral. Whenever her church was open, Elsie was there.

Elsie had an amazingly strong faith—the kind that even trusted God to do miracles. Recent tests had shown Margaret was in deep physical trouble—spots on her lungs compounded by a history of malaria. But instead of being anxious about it, her mom simply prayed that God would heal her. He did! Margaret's next physical exam revealed no spots at all. She was completely healthy. Without realizing what was taking place, Margaret was learning something about trusting God, before she even knew what that meant and before she realized how much she would need that trust later on.

In New Orleans, Margaret "sort of" entered into a relationship with the Lord. At church one day she responded to an invitation to give her life to Christ. Unfortunately, she didn't know what that meant and received no teaching to help her. Even though she was baptized the following week, her lifestyle remained unchanged.

Shortly afterward, a man named Galen Pearson entered her life. At first she thought she had zero interest in him, but within two months they were married. World War II had just gotten underway, and they weren't sure what the future might hold. As it turned out, within two short months of the wedding, Galen shipped off to serve as a gunner on a subchaser. He did not return for two and one-half years.

When Margaret received a telegram informing her that Galen was being sent to a naval hospital in Oakland, California, she wasn't even sure she wanted to be with him. He was her husband, to be sure, but he was also a stranger. It would be so much more comfortable simply to remain with her relatives in New Orleans.

After much cajoling on the part of her sister, Margaret reluctantly joined her husband. He had developed a blood clot which caused major damage to his heart. As a result he was medically discharged from the Navy, and he and his bride moved to his home state of Washington and the little town of Woodland.

Over the next several years Margaret and Galen experienced some tremendous highs and some crushing lows. Though he was supposed to take it easy, he got a job delivering milk and developed a little farm on the side. Thus, almost overnight, this society belle was transformed into a farm wife. She had no idea what she was doing. She once informed Galen that it was a real stroke of luck that he had developed ulcers in the Navy which earned him a pension, because otherwise he would have gotten ulcers from her cooking and they'd have gotten nothing out of it!

One day some neighbors invited her to the little Nazarene church in town, and she thought she would like to go. Galen refused to darken the doors of the place, however, since it was known as an assembly of "Holy Rollers." So one day when Galen was working, Margaret attended church with her neighbors.

It was there that she entered into a genuine relationship with the Lord. When she went forward, someone both prayed with her and helped her understand her faith in Jesus Christ. More than that, they came alongside her and helped her grow in her Christian life.

As it turned out, the church's reputation was well-founded. They *were* Holy Rollers—especially Grandma Taylor. Getting "blessed" frequently, she was both a hankie waver and a shouter. She would shout out her "Amen!" with the best of them. But at the same time it was obvious that she had an intimate relationship with the Lord. When she prayed the very gates of heaven seemed to swing wide open. And there was something about that praying that drew Margaret to her side like metal filings to a magnet. She just snuggled up in the arms of that 80-plus-year-old saint and soaked in everything she could.

It took some five years for Galen to enter into a relationship with Christ, but when he did, he took off like a rocket. Immediately he was up to his neck doing whatever he could do. He became the church treasurer and director of a midweek children's ministry.

Galen and Margaret fell so in love with those little ones that soon they adopted a son, Tim. Five years later, they adopted another son, Tom. They considered those two boys a blessing and poured themselves into growing them up to love and trust the Lord.

As time passed, Margaret continued to develop her ability to listen to the voice of God. Her story would remind you of the prophet Samuel. First she wasn't able to recognize the voice of God when she was spoken to. Over time, however, she came to be able to discern that voice and act on what she heard.

In April of 1974, Margaret felt impressed to give up her responsibilities at church so that she could spend more time with her husband. She did so under the protest of her pastor, who didn't want to lose such a dedicated worker. This time her listening to God was right on target, however; in October of the same year, Galen passed away.

Margaret's boys reacted quite differently to the loss of their dad. The younger one didn't really understand what had happened, but the older one did. When Margaret held Tim in her arms, he wept and his heart beat wildly like that of a little bird imprisoned in a human hand. His dad was gone, and he didn't know what to do.

From that point on, it was as if all hell broke loose. Margaret had to undergo surgery for a possible malignancy. Tim broke his leg. Tom was hospitalized for pneumonia, and they discovered their insurance had lapsed. The oil furnace failed and had to be replaced. The electric stove died in a shower of sparks. Finally, the washer gave up the ghost. After a while, there was nothing left to break.

What else was there to do but to draw even closer to the Lord? While some might shake their fists toward heaven and scream, "God, why aren't You helping me? Where are You when I need You?" Margaret would pray until she knew that she had touched the heart of God. When that happened, His peace would envelop her like a flood. Then she was equipped to face whatever lay before her.

Living on a small Social Security benefit, Margaret moved the family into Vancouver, a larger town nearby, and immediately became active in a church. As before, she did anything that was asked of her. She did much of the calling for the church, including visiting the jails. Who would have predicted that this belle from Latin America would someday minister to a woman who had pumped five bullets into her husband?

One day a life-changing letter arrived in the mail. It was from Wayne Loos, a recent widower and mountainman from Wyoming. He had been encouraged to write to Margaret by a pastor who was a mutual friend. Would she be willing for him to come to Washington to meet her?

Over my dead body! she thought . . . until God woke her up at 2 A.M. with the phrase: "Answer the letter!" A serious relationship developed after Wayne's visit, and soon the resident of Washington became a resident of Wyoming.

With her new husband came his two children, a boy named Leonard and a toddler named Joy. Margaret had her work cut out for her.

The newlyweds immediately threw themselves into the Lord's work in their church. Again, Margaret did whatever needed doing, wherever she could serve. God had prepared her for all of this, so there wasn't much she couldn't do or wasn't willing to try. It was a new twist when the high schoolers cranked up their amplifiers in her basement, but she managed to get used even to that.

Things were moving beautifully until disaster struck again. Her son Tom suddenly developed and died of acute pancreatitis. Losing Galen had been hard enough—but now Tom! Exactly five months later, her son Tim was killed in an automobile accident. And that was just the beginning.

In rapid succession, Wayne's mother died, then his father. Finally, Wayne himself died from a kind of blood poisoning. Joy responded just as Tim had when his father had died. She crawled into Margaret's arms and her heart beat wildly. What were they going to do?

Again Margaret found herself a widow with two small children. All she could do was trust the Lord. He was all they had! They all learned how to lean on the Lord as never before, and how very faithful He proved to be. The bellowing winds may have howled against them, but as long as they nestled under the Lord's wings, they would be safe.

About two years later, Leonard went rabbit hunting with a friend from church and was accidentally shot and killed. Margaret fled to her bedroom, tears streaming down her face, and cried out to God: "God, I don't understand any of this, but I have trusted You for a long time and I have loved You for a long time. I want You to know that I trust You now. I love You now."

Margaret had learned long before how to see God's light in a world filled with darkness. As she said, either she believed God was who He said He was, or she didn't. Either she believed He would do what He said He would do, or she didn't. And she believed!

Following God's leading, Margaret put her house up for sale in a time and place where such a sale seemed impossible. Yet in no time at all, the house sold. She continued to follow His lead back to Vancouver. Now she had a daughter, a small nest egg from the sale of her house, and a future that was as clear as mud. Although she did not know what the future held, she knew Who held the future, so she moved into it with confidence.

As the years went by, the prayer that had begun long ago with Grandma Taylor became the centerpiece of her life. One hour a day turned to two, then four, and sometimes to six or seven. Someone from the outside might have concluded she was just withdrawing from reality. In fact, she was plunging into the center of God's calling on her life. He had wired her to pray, and pray she did.

Margaret had a special burden to pray for church leadership, no doubt from having been brought into this world by a fallen clergyman and from having worked side by side with various pastors in a variety of churches. She understood feet of clay and the pressure designed to smash those feet. She could go right to the heart of God with clarity and compassion borne only by those who have been there.

Further, because she had experienced more sorrow than most would ever know, she could identify with and lift up the needs of those who were hurting. When they didn't know how to pray, she did. She prayed hour after hour, day after day.

God continued to be faithful to Margaret. He saw her daughter through college and met all their needs year after year. No matter what the necessity, God truly was the "Father of the fatherless."

As her daughter grew up through all these difficulties, Margaret used to say to her half-seriously: "Joy, if the Lord allows me to live until you get married, I'm going to dance at your wedding!"

And, of course, He did. So did she! Can you blame her for leaping to her feet on the wings of joy when her daughter and son-in-law said, "I do"? Can you fault her for twirling in place and shaking that tambourine with a smile so wide it brought a bright new source of light into the room?

Is Margaret wired to win? You bet! Is she winning? You better believe it! You see, I'm her pastor. I watched her dance down the aisle at that wedding and I shouted "Amen!" along with her as the tears streamed down my face. My family and I are the recipients of many of those prayers that are lifted up in the still of the night when the rest of the world is fast asleep. Margaret is wired to win. And is she ever winning!

What's Wrong with What's Right?

Margaret's life stands out because she has risen above the things that should have sunk her. She has gone through more sorrow and stress than most of us will face in a lifetime, yet has emerged on the other side smiling. David's words in Psalm 30:11,12 come to mind when I think of Margaret:

> You turned my wailing into dancing; you removed my sackcloth and clothed me with joy, that my heart may sing to you and not be silent. O Lord my God, I will give you thanks forever (NIV).

The light of God's love has surrounded Margaret like a fortress; it has obliterated the darkness that threatened her joy.

What an inspiration it is to see a life completely given over to God! What a pleasure to watch a person serve the Lord in the precise way that she was designed to do!

Sadly, strong devotion like Margaret's is considered by some to be a weakness or sickness. Chapter 8 outlined what bothers these folks. The concept of addiction to God offends them because it smacks of pathological or dysfunctional behavior.

When you take a good look at what these writers say, however, you find that it isn't really addiction to God that's the problem. What they really object to is being bound by inappropriate guilt or blind allegiance to some self-aggrandizing guru. And they *should* object to those things. There is no question that people destroy themselves by getting hooked on such things.

Many of us know someone who has fallen into the clutches of a cult and have seen the wreckage that has resulted in family relationships, careers, and even to physical health. An acquaintance of mine was so enmeshed in a cult for such a long time that his health was damaged irreparably. His body simply fell apart after lengthy periods of fasting followed by unhealthy eating. The injured organs cannot be repaired. All this happened because he chose to give himself unreservedly to a cult.

This is religious addiction at its worst. But it must not be confused with being addicted to the God who has revealed Himself in Jesus Christ! My friend will tell you that. It was only when he surrendered himself to the God who presents Himself through Jesus Christ in the Bible that his life got back on track.

Addiction Through the Airwaves

Since we're talking about negative religious addictions, allow me to give some free advice. I know of far too many well-meaning believers who are hooked on some of the evangelists who hit the TV trail. My advice: Steer clear!

The network show "Prime Time Live" recently did an exposé that showed just how out of hand things can get when people naively follow the leading of individuals who promote their own personal programs and goals. That program uncovered several areas of grave concern to all of us.

The exposé included interviews with some who claimed they were healed during an evangelist's service. Anyone watching the service would have been impressed by the miracles God allegedly performed live and in color. When questioned, however, those who supposedly had been healed admitted they had never been ill, or crippled, or paralyzed. In one case, a fellow who threw away his crutches in the service later revealed that the crutches hadn't even belonged to him. The true owner was the man seated next to him. The "healed" man didn't even seem fazed by the fraud he had helped perpetrate. "Why, I was just in the flow," he enthused.

One of the most distressing shots in the program was that of a dumpster in Oklahoma which overflowed with prayer requests for a television "ministry" out of Texas. Some of those prayer concerns tore my heart out. But much worse was the discovery that these requests never made it to those who had promised to "pray over them." Instead, the envelopes went directly to a bank where the checks were removed and deposited in the account of the television ministry. The envelopes, prayer requests, and other wastepaper were summarily thrown in the trash.

The exposé even contained some entertainment value. Chief in this category was the explanation by one evangelist for his rather obvious face-lift. He revealed to the faithful that he had spent so many hours on his hands and knees literally on top of their requests, crying over them, that his tears had released chemicals from the envelopes which in turn had caused his eyes to bag. Hence, he had no choice but to have them lifted.

The extraordinary thing is that people actually get caught up in this stuff. They continue to watch these men of the cashmere cloth and contribute to their support. Even though they don't get healed and don't get rich and their lives don't turn around, they continue their blind allegiance. Perhaps they just need to turn up their faith a notch, make another pledge, another vow, another gift. And the beat goes on!

The audience demographics of these televangelists generally describe an uneducated, unsophisticated, and undiscerning flock. Don't misunderstand. They are not stupid, but rather tend to be more trusting of those who claim spiritual authority. They are less skeptical and critical. And the bank accounts of the televangelists suggest their target audience responds big-time!

Certainly there are good pastors who teach on television. They are people of integrity, doing their very best to present God's truth so that other people might come to faith in Jesus Christ. It would be unconscionable to tar them with the same brush as those who make millions off the gospel of God's love and grace.

It's not terribly hard to tell the difference between the wolves and the shepherds. Ask a few simple questions and you'll see the differences clearly.

- To whom is attention consistently being called, to God or to the man?
- In whom is trust being placed, in God or in the man?
- On what kind of foundation is one's life being placed, God's Word or a man's formulas?
- How much airtime is given to God, and how much to gifts for the ministry?
- Is God represented as One who owns the cattle on a thousand hills, or as one teetering on the brink of bankruptcy who won't make it unless the listener responds rapidly and generously?

When folks get caught up in this warped understanding of faith in God, certainly it's destructive. But that is not addiction to God! It is addiction to a caricature of God. It is addiction to a manipulative scheme perpetrated in God's name. But don't throw the baby out with the bath water!

Dishwater Is Good Lukewarm; Faith Isn't

Much of today's literature on "toxic faith" or "religious addiction" touts lukewarm faith as a healthy thing. These authors end up so afraid of an involvement with God that is "too much" that they push for a diluted relationship with Christ. If you take their advice seriously, however, you end up with a tepid and nauseating faith in Christ.

Let's get down to basics. To be "sort of sold-out" to Christ has much in common with being "sort of pregnant"; neither is possible. Do you recall Christ's evaluation of the church at Laodicea presented in Revelation 3:15,16? "I know your works, that you are neither cold nor hot. I could wish you were cold or hot. So then, because you are lukewarm, and neither cold nor hot, I will spew you out of My mouth."

Consider some of the current literature advocating a lukewarm approach to faith in Christ. Leo Booth, an Episcopalian clergyman, defines religious addiction and addicts in these terms:

> Religious addiction entails using God, a religion, or a belief system as a means both to escape or avoid painful feelings and to seek self-esteem. It involves adopting a rigid belief system that specifies only one right way, which you feel you must force onto others by means of guilt, shame, fear, brain-washing, and elitism.[1]

Certainly some have "used" God to avoid dealing with reality. On the other hand, throughout the Bible you find God bidding His people to come to Him when they're down, in trouble, hurting, or in pain. He says that He will be a "hiding place" for His people, a refuge in a time of storm. Is it wrong to take Him at His word?

Further, Jesus says, "I am the way, the truth, and the life. No one comes to the Father except through Me" (John 14:6). Sounds pretty exclusive to me. There aren't too many ways to look at this without calling it "absolutist." He either *is* the Way or He *isn't*. And if He is, then that precludes all others.

Rev. Booth, however, thinks that such a conviction makes one an elitist and that this, in turn, is unhealthy. In his judgment we need to have a subdued, generic, and malleable faith in God. Anything with real definition and direction would risk pathology!

A more frontal attack on God-addiction is found in the book *Toxic Faith*. After insisting that any addiction is pathological, the authors say: "When a person would sacrifice family, job, economic security, and sanity for the sake of a substance, relationship, or behavior, addiction exists."[2]

Freeze that statement in your mind. As you hold it there, compare it to the following words of Jesus:

> And everyone who has left houses or brothers or sisters or father or mother or wife or children or lands, for My name's sake, shall receive a hundred-fold, and inherit everlasting life (Matthew 19:29).

> If anyone desires to come after Me, let him deny himself, and take up his cross daily, and follow Me. For whoever desires to save his life will lose it, but whoever loses his life for My sake will save it (Luke 9:23,24).

> Then he said to another, "Follow Me." But he said, "Lord, let me first go and bury my father." Jesus said to him, "Let the dead bury their own dead, but you go and preach the kingdom of God." And another also said, "Lord, I will follow You, but let me first go and bid them farewell who are at my house." But Jesus said to him, "No one, having put his hand to the plow, and looking back, is fit for the kingdom of God" (Luke 9:59-62).

You tell me: How do the authors' statements stack up to those of Jesus? While these authors are uncomfortable with strong devotion to God, Jesus says that anything less isn't enough. Anything less is unworthy of Him. In fact, He goes much further. He says that unless you are willing to surrender everything to Him, you will never find the fulfillment you seek. You will *never* win.

That is precisely the point He drove home so forcefully to the rich young ruler who came to Him asking about gaining eternal life. "If you want to be perfect [to win], go, sell what you have and give to the poor, and you will have treasure in heaven; and come, follow Me" (Matthew 19:21).

You've heard the expression "too much of a good thing." That may apply to many good things in life, from sunshine to hot-fudge sundaes. What starts out as a healthy outing or a delicious treat can lead to a bad sunburn or a stomachache if overdone. But God isn't like the sun or the sundae! You can't overdo your faith in God. If He is your source of meaning and fulfillment, you can't get too much of Him. Truly, "in Him we live and move and have our being" (Acts 17:28).

Was Paul Dysfunctional?

In an appendix at the end of *Toxic Faith*, the authors present a questionnaire to help you determine whether you are a religious addict, and hence determine whether you need help. If you respond affirmatively to at least three of their yes-or-no questions, you're in trouble. You're at least on your way to becoming a religious addict.

If you were to alter some of the questions slightly to make them more culturally relevant to the first century A.D., it's instructive to put the apostle Paul through their grid. How do you think Paul would have responded to the following sampling of questions? Would he have answered "yes" or "no"?

- Has your family complained that you are always "ministering" instead of spending time with them?
- Do you feel extreme guilt for "forsaking the assembling of the faithful, such as is the habit of some"?
- Do you find yourself with little time for the pleasure of earlier years because you are so busy "ministering"?
- Have people complained that you use so much Scripture in your conversation that it is hard to communicate with you?
- Do you regularly believe God is communicating with you in an audible voice?

There's little doubt Paul would have answered yes to all of the above without a moment's hesitation. In fact, he could have come up with questions that would have made these look like mere child's play. ("Have you willingly been beaten, flogged, shipwrecked, stoned, gone naked, been thrown in prison, placed in stocks, or chosen poverty, simply to spend more time preaching the gospel?") But because he would have answered "yes" to at least three of these questions, Paul would have had to call 1-800-227-LIFE for help.

Why would he have found himself in such a fix? Because by these authors' standards he was simply too tied up with God. He was too consumed by Christ. His life would definitely have been out-of-balance. Better for him to have spent some of that ministry time coaching a Little League team or perhaps doing a little windsurfing or working on his three-iron. Better for him to have pursued his hobby of choice than to have been a God-addict!

But he didn't. He was a God-addict, and that's why he accomplished what he did for the Lord. That's why he was able to pass so much on to you and me. He found himself because he gave himself away. He won the race because he was willing to give up his life for Christ! He found the fulfillment he sought because he lost himself in the Lord.

Will this addiction cause you to withdraw from the world? Quite the contrary. It will plunge you into it. Why? Because you will desire to be where the Lord is. And He spends His time with those who hurt. At the beginning of His ministry, Jesus quoted Isaiah to describe the work He was called to do:

> The Spirit of the Lord is upon Me, because He has anointed Me to preach the gospel to the poor. He has sent Me to heal the brokenhearted, to preach deliverance to the captives and recovery of sight to the blind, to set at liberty those who are oppressed, to preach the acceptable year of the Lord (Luke 4:18).

Thus the more you go after God, the deeper you will move a world filled with hurting people. You can't help it!

In addition, as you truly submit your life to following God's Word, you will find true balance. God and God alone can lead you into the balance that you so desire. And He presents that balance clearly and forcefully in His Word.

So what's wrong with what's right? Nothing. Some people don't want to handle it because it's so radically different from the business-as-usual, don't-get-too-excited-about-Jesus approach to life. I hope that's not true for you! I hope you're not willing to settle for lukewarm faith, for being second-best, for merely finishing the race long after the crowd has gone home.

There may be folks who have a hard time with addiction to God. They see more wrong than right in being hooked on Jesus. But the truth is, you'll never find what you seek until you become, like Paul, absolutely yielded to Christ.

The Worker

Mossyrock had never seen a title fight like this. It wasn't the "Thrilla in Manila," but it was about as close as a town of fewer than 600 would ever see. Besides, the outcome looked to be a slaughter!

In one corner, weighing in at several thousand pounds, was a committee led by the local superintendent of schools. Pound for pound, Lewis Duncan was about as tough as they came. Well-known throughout educational circles all over Washington state as a man who knew how to consolidate small, rural schools into larger ones by means of busing, he had built the local school population until it was larger than the town itself. With a student count of more than 700, Duncan thus represented quite an influential group. He was truly a person to be reckoned with. When Duncan talked, people listened. His group packed a wallop, be it political, social, or financial.

In the other corner, weighing considerably less, was the board of elders of the local community church. Although one businessman sat on the board, it was made up primarily of loggers. Their lack of education and sophistication would prove painfully obvious in any battle they might undertake with Duncan and his followers. It didn't take a genius to figure out that their clocks were about to be cleaned.

And the point of the fight? Why was it taking place? Because Duncan and his group had decided that the new pastor of the little country church needed to leave. Though the young man hadn't been in town even a year, they reckoned that was about 11 months too long.

Somehow during the process of interviewing it had slipped by Duncan and his friends that this young pastor was highly committed to teaching the Bible. While they had assumed he would be interested in the social issues of the day as well as in various types and styles of literature, he only wanted to teach the Bible straight—even with references to the original languages! Let's be honest: While learned, the man was a plain, old-fashioned, garden-variety fundamentalist. How could he ever attract the thinking, intellectually oriented crowd to the church?

Since Duncan and a number of his teachers were members of the little church, and since it was time for the annual review of the pastor's "call," they decided it was time to make their move. They would act as one, with Duncan as their spokesman. With his eloquence and political savvy, his opponents wouldn't stand a chance.

As the meeting began on that fateful Sunday afternoon, the picturesque little church crackled with tension. Faces that normally wore warm smiles were now taut and dry. The gentle greetings which usually made you feel so comfortable had become short and stilted. Everyone knew this was going to be unlike the annual church picnic.

But Duncan and his henchmen hadn't counted on one slight wrinkle. A few weeks before the meeting was to take place, young Pastor Goodrick had caught wind of what was being planned. Because he was inexperienced in things like this, he had no clue how to respond. So, with no one else to turn to, he decided to take the information to his board of elders. At least they could pray with him about it. Who knows? They might even have some good ideas about what to do.

As various options were considered, Pastor Goodrick knew he wasn't interested in a fight. He didn't want this to turn into an us-against-them confrontation. After all, it could be that he really shouldn't stay on as pastor. Maybe what this group was saying was true, that he wasn't doing the job that needed to be done.

With that in mind, he asked the board to do just one thing in preparation for the annual meeting. He wanted them to prepare an honest evaluation of his year's efforts as their pastor. He wanted them to be honest and thorough, pulling no punches. He wanted them to examine his character and contribution in light of what Scripture taught about pastors. If they would just do that, he was willing to let the chips fall where they might.

As the meeting itself unfolded, nobody was quite ready for what happened. After the perfunctory details of business were dispensed with, they got to the main event. What an event it proved to be!

The showdown began when Neal Kjesbu stood up to represent the board of elders. Neal Kjesbu. Even though he was chairman of the board, he was hardly a worthy opponent for someone like Lewis Duncan. Kjesbu was a simple stump-farmer and part-time mailman. Although he had wanted to be a minister, he had been forced to drop out of Bible school due to some sort of physical malady and thus never received any degree. It had been a challenge for him and his family merely to survive on the earnings of his little farm and his mail route that he ran only once every three days.

Oh, Kjesbu was well-liked, to be sure. You wouldn't be pushing it too far to say he was highly respected. There was something about his integrity, his gentleness, and his unmatched love for people that made him stand head and shoulders above most other men.

But if you used the normal standards of evaluation, you could hardly call Neal a success. Certainly he had never attained fame or fortune, and his possibilities in that regard didn't look too promising.

The fact is, however, that Neal was an incredible man. Tucked neatly under that gentle spirit was a giant of a man, a man bathed in the Spirit of God. Maybe it was because God was the beginning, end, and middle of his life. Maybe it was because he immersed himself in the Word, never reading his Bible less than twice a day. Or just maybe it was because he was committed to expressing his faith in every area of his life.

Whatever it was that accounted for his style, Neal was cut from a different bolt of cloth than most folks. If you were to sum up his life in one word, it would have been *worker*.

After returning to the farm from Bible school and realizing that the rest of his life would probably be spent there, Neal set about to honor the Lord and bless others with whatever skills and resources he possessed. Being a jack-of-all-trades, it was just as common for Neal to help someone with a roof as it was to fix a broken pipe. He served with boundless energy, taking no pay for his efforts.

When he ran his mail route through the hills on Mondays, he often would find notes in mailboxes asking him to pick up something at the local mercantile store where most folks in the area had accounts. Then on Thursday, while his mail was being sorted, he would swing his old panel truck over to the store, fill each request, load the supplies into the truck with the mail, and deliver them along the route. What might have been a burden for other people was a blessing for Neal. He was exactly where he was supposed to be, and he loved it!

Because some Chinook Indians on his route couldn't read English, Neal learned how to speak Chinook. That way he could help them meet the needs that cropped up in their lives, as well as encourage them along the way.

On occasions too numerous to mention Neal extended himself to somebody who was ill. Whether it was someone along his mail route, a member of his church, or one of the folks in the community at large, he would make a home visit, usually bringing with him one of his children and his guitar. After praying for the one who was infirm, he would then encourage the person with a song or two.

On Sundays, after attending the little community church, he would rush the family home, grab a bite to eat, load everyone into his panel truck, and drive to the community of

Harmony where he would conduct a Sunday school for anyone in the area who desired to attend. Sunday after Sunday, year after year, he faithfully attended to this task. To him it wasn't a chore; it was a joy. He felt it was a real treat to be able to teach other people the Word of God.

If ever anyone bore a full crop of the fruit of the Spirit, it was Neal Kjesbu. As he served others with the joy of the Lord, they grew to trust and love him greatly.

Thus, when Neal Kjesbu stood to represent the board of elders in that difficult Sunday afternoon meeting, it became clear that his presence and stature had been overlooked. His soft-spoken, gentle-yet-firm voice disarmed the crowd.

A man of few words, he commanded attention as he went right to the point. He told the people that he was going to give an evaluation of the pastor, and that is exactly what he proceeded to do. In words more glowing than the pastor himself could have imagined, Neal painted the portrait of a near-saint. Listing one good attribute after another, he pointed out that in his humble opinion, the citizens of Mossyrock and surrounding communities were fortunate indeed to have someone of the caliber of Rev. Goodrick. Because of his faithfulness to teach the unchangeable truths of God, Neal testified that he had learned things he had never before known. And he was certain that they had seen only the tip of the iceberg.

Ending his speech with a hearty recommendation that they keep the pastor another year, Neal quietly took his seat.

The room went silent. Tension had increased by a factor of ten. What would happen now?

After what seemed like an eternity, Lewis Duncan rose to his feet. He headed the team that wanted to dismiss the pastor and he would now bring his organizational efforts to their conclusion. Confrontation and pressure were hardly new to him, and he had opposed very eloquent and learned men numerous times. But never before had he faced someone with the character and commitment of Neal Kjesbu. Never had he come face-to-face with someone so free from guile, so desirous merely to serve his God.

His testimony was considerably shorter than Kjesbu's. "I don't know what you people think," he sputtered quickly and quietly, "but as far as I am concerned, if our pastor is good enough for Neal Kjesbu, he's good enough for me!" With that, he sat down and was silent for the duration of the meeting.

Within moments the pastor was asked overwhelmingly to stay on for another year, which ultimately turned into six. All because of one man who served the Lord with his whole heart: Neal Kjesbu.

And what became of this humble servant of God? As you might guess, he never became a man of position or possessions. He never became what he once aspired to be, a pastor. But despite that, he served the Lord as he had been designed to do and was held in high esteem by his entire community.

No doubt if you were to ask Neal himself, he would not have been aware either of his influence or his impact. Given his humility, even the discussion of it would have made him uneasy.

But the simple truth is that Neal Kjesbu was wired to win, and he won! He took what God had built into his life and pressed it fully into service for Him. As he did, God blessed and honored his commitment and used his life to accomplish great things—even unexpected things.

Just ask Lewis Duncan.

Give Yourself Away for God

Why is it that people like Billy Graham or Mother Teresa are so universally admired? Is it because they have amassed such wealth? Because of the fabulous trips they take, where the "paparazzi" catch them playing in their mountain retreats? Because of the grand restaurants they eat in or the trendsetting fashions in which they clothe themselves? Is it perhaps because they have attained and exercised such power? Because they have so many people at their beck and call? Or is it rather because they have made the choice to give themselves away for the cause of Christ? Is it because they have consciously chosen to use everything that is at their disposal to bring glory and honor to God?

These folks march to the beat of a different drummer than most of the rest of the world. That's why they stand out. That's why people notice them. That's why their influence extends far beyond what they would have been able to cultivate otherwise. They have gained tremendous joy and satisfaction in their lives because they have given so much away. And that's not all. The same thing holds true for you.

When you come to the point where you willingly and joyfully press everything you have into service for the Lord, when you willingly give whatever you are to the cause of Jesus Christ, you will find out what it feels like to win. You'll be a winner!

But until you come to this point, you will never win. Oh, you might be successful in the world's terms. You might be rich beyond measure, extremely well-known, and recognized instantly. You might even do something that causes others to remember you when you're dead and gone. But you still won't win. You won't experience the wholeness, the completion, the sense of satisfaction God has reserved just for you. It's impossible.

Why? Because you've got to give to get. That is just a principle God has built into the fabric of His universe. Sound a little farfetched? Consider what Jesus had to say about it in terms that no doubt jolted His followers.

> Do not think that I came to bring peace on earth. I did not come to bring peace but a sword. For I have come to "set a man against his father, a daughter against her mother, and a daughter-in-law against her mother-in-law." And "a man's foes will be those of his own household." He who loves father or mother more than Me is not worthy of Me. And he who loves son or daughter more than Me is not worthy of Me. And he who does not take his cross and follow after Me is not worthy of Me. He who finds his life will lose it, and he who loses his life for My sake will find it (Matthew 10:34-39).

At first glance this sounds harsh, almost brutal. Yet when you get at its essence, it all makes sense. What principles is Jesus setting forth through these words?

First, He means that real life is a function of being totally caught up in your relationship with Him. He has to be number one, ahead of everything else in your life—including your family. If that isn't true for you, forget about winning.

Recently I heard a talk by a person of some renown. As he summed up his colorful life, he stated his conclusion that family was more important than anything else in life. As long as you had your family, he said, you had everything you needed for happiness. Even if you had nothing else to your name, having a good relationship with your family would bring you all the contentment you could ever ask for.

Really? Is that true? If so, tell it to Job, who lost his whole family. If he had placed all his hope in his family, what would their loss have meant for him? To whom would he have turned when they weren't there? No, Jesus says that He must be first and foremost in your life. He must set the pace for who you are and what you do with your life.

Second, Christ is saying that until you are willing to go after your relationship with Him with abandon, you will not find the satisfaction you seek. As long as you play by your own rules, calling all the shots yourself, you will never get where you want to go. You may feel as though you are going to. But it will never happen.

Third, He is saying that the more you try to establish your own fulfillment, the quicker it will slip through your fingers. By the same token, the more you give yourself away in living for Him, the more He will fill you with the joy you so desire.

It amazes me how few Christians understand this truth. Oh, they confess a belief in Christ. At least on a verbal and intellectual level they claim He is at the center of their lives. But then they turn around and live like He doesn't exist. They chase the same things as everybody else in a vain attempt to find happiness. "Of course I love the Lord. But I just know things will go better for me when I get a new _____." Fill in the blank yourself. Be it a car, house, husband, job, or something else, the *last* thing they have in mind to find happiness is giving themselves away. But Jesus insists it's a precondition. You've got to lose to find, give to gain.

He gives the same message in Matthew 16:25,26:

> For whoever desires to save his life will lose it, and whoever loses his life for My sake will find it. For what is a man profited if he gains the whole world, and loses his own soul? Or what will a man give in exchange for his soul?

Politicians tell you that it is your inalienable right to have whatever you desire. Positive thinkers tell you that you deserve the best; just visualize it and it's yours! Business types chide you to be diligent and work hard and you can attain any goal you set for yourself. Athletes urge you to "go for the gold."

Yet Jesus says the only way to find your life is to lose it for His sake.

Somebody's got to be right, and somebody's got to be wrong. Who are you going to believe?

Finally, in what could seem like a completely unrelated teaching, Jesus comments: "No one can serve two masters; for either he will hate the one and love the other, or else he will be loyal to the one and despise the other. You cannot serve God and mammon" (Matthew 6:24).

Again, play across your mind the approach most Christians take to life. Regardless of what they say, they act as if they *can* have two masters. They think they can be totally immersed in the world and its values and totally caught up in their faith in Christ. But like Jesus said: "Not!" (Revised Ritchie translation). You're either going to give yourself to the world or you're going to give yourself away for the Lord. You can't have it both ways, regardless of what people might say.

So what does it look like to give your life away? Does it mean that you will sell all your possessions and live under a bridge? Will it relegate you to a '64 Dodge Dart with a ding on one fender and an "I love Jesus" sticker on your bumper? Does it call to mind a sea of polyester clothing with pulls and pills too numerous to mention?

These things have little to do with giving yourself away for the Lord. I suspect that if God designed you to drive a Dodge Dart, you'll have a real hankering to pilot one. But otherwise, you may even try a Ford! What kinds of physical resources you have and how you utilize them is something you need to work out with God. And just as our wiring differs from person to person, so do the physical resources we have to manage. Abraham, David, Solomon, and even Lydia had great wealth they were called upon to manage. Nowhere do we find them divesting themselves of those resources to make a statement about their love for God. Yet in all cases we find a willingness to be and do whatever it was that God desired—except Solomon. And you can read how he ended up in 1 Kings 11.

God is giving you the opportunity to thrive. You, too, can be a winner! All the stories you have read in this book about people such as Neal Kjesbu or Fanny Crosby or Margaret Loos have given you vivid illustrations of those who have learned to give themselves away. In every case, as they surrendered their lives to the Lord and allowed Him to set their pace, they found very clear direction about how they were to live. In some cases they had much materially. In other cases they had little. Some were multitalented, while others felt fortunate to have one gift. In all cases, however, they were faithful to yield everything to the Lord and give all away in His service. As a result, their lives took on a breadth and depth and richness that could only come from God Himself.

How do you give yourself away? It all depends. How has God wired you? How does that wiring best work to bless Him? It may be that you are an accountant. God has wired you to crunch numbers. There is nothing you like to do more than this. In fact, if you had the choice of working on a complex tax return or seeing a good movie, you would choose the tax return any day of the week! Further, let's assume that you make a living as an accountant. You actually get paid for doing what you were designed to do, what you love to do. In your case, your wiring happens to parallel the job by which you derive your income. How then do you press your wiring into service for the Lord?

When was the last time you asked your pastor if there were any widows in your church who had a tough time balancing their checkbooks? How often have you sought out opportunities to help young couples learn how to develop a budget and faithfully manage their monetary resources for the Lord? What steps have you taken to see how your skills might be utilized in a local youth ministry? In other words, are you so caught up in using your wiring to bless *yourself* that you haven't yet considered how it might be given away to serve *the Lord*? Remember: You'll never find fulfillment as long as you orient your life around yourself.

Or maybe you're not an accountant. Let's say you're a teacher. You have taught third grade for 15 years and it just seems to be your niche. Unlike the accountant, however, you do not particularly find joy in your vocation. Oh, you do it, and you do it rather well. But what you really like to do is sing. You may not be the greatest singer to come down the pike, but you're not bad. In fact, the people in your church love to hear you sing. They look forward to it. Whenever you step out of the choir and take the microphone, they just know something powerful is coming. And you feel the same way. Something indescribable happens between the Lord and you whenever you sing for Him. You get blessed. He gets blessed. The people get blessed. Everybody wins.

So what do you do? Quit teaching and move to Nashville? Or find opportunities in nursing homes and new church start-ups and home Bible studies and worship groups to lift your voice in praise to the Lord? Just because you derive your income from something other than singing doesn't mean you can't give yourself away in song to glorify God.

Or what if you happen to put bread on the table as a landscaper, but really are a servant like some of the people mentioned earlier? How might you use your skills and interests in landscaping to serve the Lord? Might you also invest your service in helping in the nursery at church, cooking for an all-church picnic, or directing traffic at a Billy Graham crusade? Would you find it meaningful to be a good male role model for the eight-year-old son of a single-parent mom in your church? Could you direct a fleet of other volunteers who would be willing to repair house problems for the elderly and shut-ins?

I hope you're beginning to catch the drift of all of this. Open your mind to consider the myriad ways in which you might press your wiring into full service to glorify the Lord. Do you see that as you do so, you will be blessed and fulfilled yourself? Do you understand what an encouragement you will be to other people as they see you giving yourself away?

The idea is not that you must be in "full-time Christian service" to *really* serve God. I'm not sure I even know what "full-time Christian service" is. You either are serving the

Lord or you aren't. You either give yourself away for Him or you don't. But you don't serve Him part-time. The whole idea of "Christian" vocations makes little sense to me. If you are a Christian and have a vocation, then you have a Christian vocation! Though I may get my paycheck from a church and you from being a veterinarian, if we are both Christians, we are both in Christian vocations. The question is not what we do, it is how we serve the Lord where we are. Wherever we are, we can either give ourselves away for God or do our job with an eye only toward self-interest.

Don't get caught up in the "religious ghetto" kind of thinking which reserves service to God to ecclesiastical vocations. If that is the only way to give yourself away to God, then not even the apostle Paul pulled it off. In fact, if working in a church or related institution is the only way to serve God fully, then you rule out most of the early church.

When Paul hit a new town, he asked two questions:

- Who needs to know about Jesus?
- Who needs a new tent?

The way he financially provided for himself was only a means to an end. It was never an end in itself. The "end" of his life was rather giving himself away for God. Thus, given his unique wiring, he invested himself in spreading the gospel all over the ancient Near East. He feared no one, nor any new situation. He was prepared to take on all comers and did so with abandon. Consequently, God used him mightily.

Paul was never meant to be the exception to the rule! He was rather meant to illustrate the rule. The more you give, the more you get. The more you lose, the more you find. The greater your investment, the greater your return. Only when you give yourself away for God do you ever find true abundance in living.

Something other than complete surrender may bring you momentary satisfaction. It may even bring you fleeting pleasure. But it will never bring you contentment or joy. It can't! God didn't design things to work that way.

Instead, He planned it so that you must put everything on the table for Him. You must step out of your comfort zone and make a leap of faith, believing that He will bless your faithfulness to follow Him.

So take the plunge! Risk it! Once you've discovered how you are wired and learned to delight in it, press everything you have and are into service for the Lord. It is the only way to win!

Runners,
to Your Marks!

If you're alive, you are wired to win. God designed you for that from the beginning. But maybe you haven't realized it until now. Maybe too many other things have gotten in the way. Perhaps you've taken too many detours over muddy roadways. It's quite possible that, in reading the stories in this book of those who are wired to win and are winning, you have thought, *But they are such dynamic people! Of course they can win! Why not? They've got all the right equipment. They're charismatic, brilliant, confident, and capable. But not me. I'm just plain vanilla. No way could I ever be like them. None of them describes me!*

If you call working half-time as a stump farmer and the other half-time as a rural route postman "dynamic," then I guess Neal Kjesbu was. If you consider fighting ill health through much of your life, losing two husbands and four sons "dynamic," then perhaps that's a good description of Margaret Loos. But the simple truth is this: Whenever you give yourself away for the Lord, your life *is* going to be dynamic.

151

You *are* going to be in a special class of people. You *will* find joy and excitement and challenge and fullness, the likes of which isn't approachable elsewhere. In other words, you will be winning!

God didn't design you merely to finish. He has made available to you everything it takes to win. Become consumed by Christ, a true God-addict. Discover how He has uniquely wired you. Delight in it completely. Then press everything you have into service for Him. As you do, surely you will be the next chapter in this book, for you will be a winner, too!

On your mark, get set, GO!

NOTES

CHAPTER 2

1. Here are several books to help readers get a handle on their spiritual gifts. While the authors differ somewhat in their theology, all provide helpful guidance in this important pursuit. I would recommend:

   Tim Blanchard, *Finding Your Spiritual Gifts* (Wheaton, IL: Tyndale House, 1983).

   Don and Katie Fortune, *Discover Your God-Given Gifts* (Tarrytown, NY: Fleming H. Revell, 1987).

   Ken Hemphill, *Mirror, Mirror on the Wall* (Nashville: Broadman Press, 1992).

2. Paul Pearsall, *Super-Joy* (New York: Bantam Books, 1988), p. 45.
3. Howard Gardner, *Frames of Mind* (New York: Basic Books, 1985), p. 59.
4. Ibid., pp. 8-9.
5. Chuck Colson and Jack Eckerd, *Why America Doesn't Work* (Dallas: Word Publishing, 1991), p. 92.
6. John Bradley and Jay Carty, *Unlocking Your Sixth Suitcase* (Colorado Springs: NavPress, 1991).
7. Arthur F. Miller and Ralph T. Mattson, *The Truth About You* (Berkeley: Ten Speed Press, 1989).

CHAPTER 4

1. "The Applause of Heaven and Earth" *Leadership Journal*, Summer 1992, Vol. 13, No. 3.

CHAPTER 7

1. Bernard Ruffin, *Fanny Crosby* (New York: Pilgrim Press, 1976), p. 24.
2. Ray Beeson and Ranelda Hunsicker, *The Hidden Price of Greatness* (Wheaton, IL: Tyndale House, 1991), p. 88.
3. Kenneth W. Osbeck, *101 Hymns* (Grand Rapids: Kregel Publications, 1982), p. 167.

4. Ruffin, *Fanny Crosby,* p. 68.
5. Kenneth Osbeck, *101 More Hymn Stories* (Grand Rapids: Kregel Publications, 1985), p. 240.
6. Ibid., p. 240.
7. Ruffin, *Fanny Crosby,* pp. 88-89.
8. Osbeck, *101 More Hymn Stories*, p. 237.
9. *Fanny J. Crosby, An Autobiography* (Grand Rapids: Baker Book House, 1906), p. 195.
10. Ruffin, *Fanny Crosby,* p. 15.
11. Ruffin, *Fanny Crosby,* p. 13.
12. Charles Simeon, *Evangelical Preaching* (Portland: Multnomah Press, 1986), pp. xxviii-xxix.
13. Ibid., p. xxx.
14. Ibid.

CHAPTER 8

1. Ray Beeson and Ranelda Mack Hunsicker, *The Hidden Price of Greatness* (Wheaton, IL: Tyndale House, 1991), pp. 3-7.
2. Paul Pearsall, *Super-Joy* (New York: Bantam Books, 1988), p. 209.
3. George H. Gallup, Jr., and Timothy Jones, *The Saints Among Us* (Harrisburg: Morehouse Publishing, 1992), p. 87.
4. Dennis C. Daley, *Kicking Addictive Habits Once and for All* (Lexington: Lexington Books, 1991), p. 6.
5. Anne Wilson Schaef, *Escape From Intimacy* (San Francisco: Harper & Row, 1989), p. 9.
6. Ibid., p. 10.
7. Stephen Arterburn and Jack Felton, *Toxic Faith* (Nashville: Oliver Nelson, 1991), p. 104.
8. William F. Arndt and F. Wilbur Gingrich, *A Greek-English Lexicon of the New Testament* (Chicago: University of Chicago Press, 1957), pp. 204-205.
9. John W. Styll, "What's New?" *Contemporary Christian Music*, Nov. 1991, p. 54.

CHAPTER 11

1. "Dial 'R' For Revolution," *The Oregonian*, Aug. 2, 1992, L10.
2. Harvey Milkman and Stanley Sunderwirth, *Craving for Ecstasy* (Lexington: Lexington Books, 1987), p. 6.
3. Paul Pearsall, *Super-Joy* (New York: Bantam Books, 1988), p. 10.
4. William Glasser, *Positive Addiction* (New York: Harper & Row, 1976), pp. 63-66.

5. Norman Cousins, *Head First* (New York: Penguin Books, 1989), p. 127.
6. Alan Loy McGinnis, *The Power of Optimism* (San Francisco: Harper & Row, 1990), p. 95.
7. David G. Myers, *The Pursuit of Happiness* (New York: William Morrow & Company, Inc., 1992), pp. 20-21.
8. Pearsall, p. 17.
9. Ibid., pp. 19-20.
10. Ibid., pp. 20-21.

CHAPTER 12

1. "The Trees of the Field," © 1975 by Lillenas Publishing Co. All rights reserved.

CHAPTER 13

1. Leo Booth, *When God Becomes a Drug* (Los Angeles: Jeremy P. Tarcher, Inc., 1991), p. 2.
2. Stephen Arterburn and Jack Felton, *Toxic Faith* (Nashville: Oliver Nelson, 1991), p. 104.

BILL RITCHIE

is an insightful and entertaining keynote speaker and seminar leader for corporate, institutional, public, and church audiences. He has addressed audiences across the United States and appeared on nationally broadcast television and radio programs. For further information on guest appearances and other topics, please call or write:

Bill Ritchie
Crossroads Community Church
7709 NE 78th ST
Vancouver, WA 98662
(503) 289-6302